Hal and Charlie

Hal and Charlie

The Texas Peterson Brothers
Who Risked a Fortune
For a Hill Country Foundation

By Vicki J. Audette and
J. Tom Graham

Eakin Press Fort Worth, Texas
www.EakinPress.com

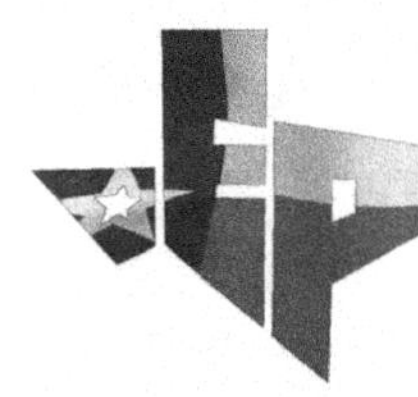

Published By Eakin Press
An Imprint of Wild Horse Media Group
P.O. Box 331779
Fort Worth, Texas 76163
1-817-344-7036
www.EakinPress.com

1 2 3 4 5 6 7 8 9
Paperback ISBN 978-1-68179-215-6

CONTENTS

PREFACE

Hal and Charlie Peterson, like so many people who have accumulated wealth, valued privacy and hid from the spotlight.

And the Hal and Charlie Peterson Foundation—which they founded, endowed, and directed in its early days—reflected this privacy for decades. Despite its lasting civic contributions to the people of the Hill Country community, the Foundation maintained a very low profile from its offices in Kerrville, Texas, until the mid-1990s.

However, in 1997, the board of directors of the Hal and Charlie Peterson Foundation realized that the history of the two founders was slowly being lost year by year as the people who knew and worked with them died. Because Hal and Charlie rarely sought or endured publicity, information about the two men is sparse.

The Peterson Foundation board members decided to commission this book to preserve what remains of the memory of Hal and Charlie, their remarkable lives, their staggering accomplishments and rare failures, and their large and perpetual gift to the Texas Hill Country.

What follows in these chapters is an effort to determine who Hal and Charlie really were and what motivated them to invest their wealth in the public good. An attempt to capture the character of these two brothers must also include the pioneer times in which they lived, the Hill Country which was their home, and the people with whom they associated.

INTRODUCTION

The Peterson Boys Go to Town

At fifteen years of age, Hal Peterson "went to town," as folks back then described leaving the farm.

To the consternation of the Sid "Cap" Peterson family, which was struggling to keep its Texas Hill Country ranch intact during the period before World War I, their oldest son embarked on his extraordinary business career at the age of fifteen from a small desk in the corner of the M. F. Weston Garage in Kerrville, Texas. Perhaps it was his destiny. After all, Cap Peterson had nicknamed his oldest son "Boss" before Hal was in long pants. And the moniker fit. "Boss" was what everyone called Hal for the remainder of his life.

After Boss left, the family still had two sons on the land. Charlie was the second son, an unusually handsome and affable youth who was two years younger than Boss. The third was Joe Sid, another two years younger than Charlie and an independent-natured kid who adapted easily to the self-reliance of a rancher.

With no time to waste on childhood, Boss purchased the Weston Garage on the corner of Water Street and Sidney Baker in downtown Kerrville at the ripe old age of eighteen. On the same spot he launched Peterson's Garage and Auto Company, which became the bedrock of a Hill Country business empire.

Before long, Charlie followed his big brother to town, and the two formed what came to be one of the most fascinating and successful unwritten business partnerships in Texas. (The youngest Peterson boy, Joe Sid, never really yearned to follow his brothers and spent his life on the family ranch.)

Hal and Charlie went on to create an enterprise called the Peterson Interests, which at its peak included twenty-two major companies worth millions by the time Hal "Boss" Peterson died in 1962. (Charlie died in 1953.)

The two brothers, through an unstated yet clearly understood gentleman's agreement, left the bulk of their estates to the Hal and Charlie Peterson Foundation, which built and supported the major medical facility in the Texas Hill Country: The Sid Peterson Memorial Hospital, named after the brothers' father, Sid "Cap" Peterson.

In the four decades since Hal and Charlie died, the Peterson Foundation has grown into the major benevolent force in the Texas Hill Country. Although no one in South Texas totally understood the brotherly agreement between Boss and Charlie, the mechanics of how this handshake partnership transpired seem even more mystical today when business agreements, even among family members, involve pages of i-dotting and t-crossing and lawyers by the score.

The eldest son of a natural gambler, Boss inherited his father's knack for horse trading and advanced it to a new level of multimillion-dollar deal making. Business associates still marvel at how the seasoned Boss would "listen" his way into a deal. A typical negotiation would go something like this:

Wearing Coke bottle-thick lenses in his eyeglasses, which made his eyes appear even bigger than they were, Boss would look holes through whoever was pitching a business venture to him. His big eyes would appear to glare without blinking. When the pitchman would explain his deal the first time, he might propose a 50-50 split. Boss would listen, say very little, and keep staring with those unblinking eyes.

Not knowing how else to break the uncomfortable silence, the pitch-man would talk through the deal again, this time proposing a 60-40 split, with Boss getting the 60 percent. Boss still would only listen with nary a blink. So the pitch-man would outline his proposal a third time, and this presentation might include a 70-30 split, with Boss getting the 70 percent.

When Boss was convinced he had heard the fellow's best offer, he would leave him with his trademark, "I'll think about it." If the deal interested Boss, the pitch-man would be given the opportunity to sell his proposal once again. If it did not, the man would never hear back from Boss.

An equal partner in Peterson Interests, brother Charlie played a completely different and much more subtle role. Boss would propose all of his business deals to Charlie, who had an equal amount of money at risk. Kerrville associates who knew the two brothers believed Charlie provided a down-to-earth anchor in contrast to Boss's high-flying visionary schemes. It was Charlie who kept the grass-root contacts and visited with the local folks, while Boss concentrated on the big picture.

Charlie's attention span for business deals was often interrupted by his zeal for Texas Hill Country living. After fifteen minutes of discussion, Charlie might say, "Do what you think, Boss. I've got to go. I've only got four more days of good deer hunting." Or he would head off for Mexico with his wife, or pursue his passion for fishing and outdoor life.

Although their style was unconventional as standard business practices go, there can be no question that it worked. Starting in the 1920s, the brothers built an ever-growing vertical line of businesses worth millions of dollars back in the days when even one dollar was hard to come by.

For decades, the brothers' relationship raised questions, even to the people who knew them best. Why, for example, didn't youngest brother Joe Sid ever participate in the partnership? Perhaps one hint to the answer came at the outset of their adult lives.

Cap Peterson is said to have given money to each of his three sons to finance a start in business. Hal and Charlie invested in automobiles and buses and thereby developed an empire. Joe Sid bought the Manhattan Cafe in downtown Kerrville, which he owned only a short time before returning to the ranch.

Joe Sid's seeming distaste for business probably worked out best for all the brothers. Most likely, the independent Joe Sid would have argued with Boss about his various ventures. On the other hand, Charlie often advised caution, but at decision time he usually trusted Boss's business instincts all the way to the bank. Call it chemistry. Every business deal was always Hal and Charlie, never

Hal and Charlie and Joe Sid, although the three remained very close throughout their lives.

From the beginning, Hal and Charlie pooled their money, and though it remained largely under Boss's control, the two brothers' fortune remained together not only through their lives but also through their deaths.

From the gentle Charlie's point of view, the off-paper partnership worked. Although Charlie never regarded money as the primary goal of his life and at times appeared to have only a passing interest in the business empire, he became equally wealthy right along with his hard-charging brother. And from Boss's point of view, the complementary partnership may have been an essential element to his success.

A true visionary, Boss could see the potential in all kinds of deals. In the Texas wheeler-dealer tradition from which giants of business and politics were born, Boss could think of more angles to pursue before breakfast than an army of his associates could execute in a decade. The even-tempered Charlie may have provided the restraint Boss required to keep his boundless energy in check.

Indeed, it appears many of the business deals were structured for just that purpose. Boss would own 49 percent, and Charlie would own 49 percent. Boss's chief lieutenant and brilliant detail man, Guy Griggs, would own the swing 2 percent. If Boss and Charlie agreed, Guy's 2 percent was meaningless. But if Boss was leaning too far out of the boat, Charlie's 49 percent and Guy's 2 percent would serve as a ballast to bring Boss back to upright.

The few failures Boss endured may have come when his impulsive nature went unchecked. The purchase of the Yellow Cab Company in Kerrville is an example. Boss was a student of the vertical integration of industries, such as Standard Oil, which tried to monopolize the energy industry from the point of removing oil from the ground to pumping it into the automobile. Boss was intent on building a vertically integrated transportation company, and a piece of that puzzle was, in his mind, the Yellow Cab Company. The acquisition made no sense to brother Charlie or to Boss's lieutenant Guy Griggs, who thought buying the cab company was such a bad idea that he refused to "look after it" as he did other Peterson businesses. The Yellow Cab Company, without Griggs's guidance, never made a profit.

Despite their successes, the two brothers carried several weighted handicaps on their backs. All the Petersons had a family history of heart disease and myriad related health problems. Boss spent so much of his life in hospitals that his friends joked that his "business suit" was a pair of pajamas and a robe.

The Petersons also had a history of drinking problems. Charlie and Boss consumed alcohol heavily every day, and Boss's associates were continually scrambling to clean up some of his late-night decisions which didn't look nearly as attractive by light of morning. Nevertheless, several noted: "Boss was smarter while tight than most men are cold sober."

If the Peterson associates at times had to compensate for the heavy drinking, they also realized that hospitality was an integral part of Boss's business strategy and success. One of the Peterson ranches, Camp Eagle, may have been the most legendary party site in the state. From the top officials at General Motors to the leading Texas and national politicians, everybody who was anybody was entertained at Camp Eagle. Getting on the guest list was considered a masterstroke. An annual invite was reserved for the business elite. Humble Oil executives enjoyed the best hunting week every year.

Boss's man Friday was named R. S. T. Walker, but Boss called him Rastus. From singing like the Ink Spots to tending bar, Rastus became a top Camp Eagle attraction.

Before Camp Eagle, Boss lived regularly in San Antonio's downtown hotels. His parties were so frequent that he was occasionally asked to move for the relief of the hotel's staff. Women found the well-groomed Charlie to be attractive. When one friend tried to introduce him to a San Antonio manicurist, he discovered she already knew of Charlie Peterson—as perhaps did most other single women in downtown San Antonio. If the balding, 200-plus-pound Boss's appeal was the air of power, the trim and shy Charlie was the nice guy with boyish charm whom women found irresistible.

Boss married three times; Charlie married twice. Both found the love of their lives: Boss with his first wife, and Charlie with his last. But neither produced a child to inherit their vast wealth. While Charlie always appeared happy, people who knew Boss best wondered if he carried a deep emptiness inside him, a loneliness which caused him to "never want to be alone."

Charlie spent the bulk of his time on family and friends, while his brother's passion was always the next business deal and the amassing of even more capital under the Peterson name. A motivation for creating the Hal and Charlie Peterson Foundation may have been, at least partially, to retain under the Peterson name the vast profits from the Kerrville Bus Company rather than see them all go to Washington via the "excess profits tax." When the Bus Company generated its first $1 million in profit, Boss and Charlie were quoted as saying that they got to keep only $17,000 each after taxes.

Boss, who spent several months out of each year in hospitals, understood the need for good medical facilities. Even though Kerrville was famed as a warm and high retreat for people who suffered with tuberculosis, the "Capital of the Texas Hill Country" had only what Boss described as a ramshackle hospital serving the townspeople, and Boss determined that a new one would be his gift to the community.

As always, Boss had a natural-born Texas streak of thinking big. He didn't just want to build a hospital. He dreamed of the "Mayo Clinic of the South." His vision pierced far beyond the view of those around him. When a young Clyde Parker had just arrived in town and purchased a lumberyard, Boss asked Clyde to investigate obtaining a steel house franchise from a company in Toledo, Ohio. Clyde questioned whether people in Kerrville would be interested in steel houses, but Boss responded: "Hell, I'm not just talking about Kerrville. I'm talking about everything west of the Mississippi."

Even though he was never formally honored by Kerrville for his community efforts, Boss promoted the city constantly and embarked on a massive campaign to locate the Air Force Academy there. He came very close.

Although Boss was too frail to hunt frequently, he was one of the pioneers who realized the economic impact which hunting would later have on the Texas Hill Country. His interest brought an appointment to the Texas Fish and Game Commission, and he was among the first wave to introduce exotic game and tall game fences to the region. When Kerrville proved too small of a playing field, Boss initiated the upscale Castle Hills development in San Antonio.

Friends often wondered how much more Boss might have

accomplished if he had not been persistently hindered by health problems.

Boss's mind was the stuff of legends, much like his father Cap's iron-trap memory. When the Castle Hills development was under way, Boss told his developer, George Delavan, to hire a Kerrville builder who owed him $8,765.43 for a bulldozer which had been sold to the builder four years earlier. George called the man to tell him he had the job, but Boss wanted the bulldozer debt paid off. George decided to test Boss's memory and asked the man to look up the exact amount of the debt. Not surprisingly, it was $8,765.43.

In the four decades since Boss and Charlie died, the Peterson Foundation and the Sid Peterson Memorial Hospital have grown into two major benevolent forces holding more than $100 million in assets.

The legendary Peterson brothers, who seldom saw their names in print, left a legacy which becomes more valuable to the Texas Hill Country every year.

The Sid Peterson Family. Front row (left to right) Sid "Cap" Peterson, Myrta Peterson, Hal "Boss" Peterson. Back row (left to right) Charlie Peterson and Joe Sid Peterson.

Part One

The Roots

The Peterson extended family photo shows Hal, Charlie, and Joe Sid as boys. Joe Sid is seated with arms folded in front row; next to him (with head down) is Charlie. In the second row, last on right (also with head bowed) is Hal "Boss" Peterson.

CHAPTER 1

The Legacy

ONE OF THE MOST dynamic men the Texas Hill Country ever produced suffered from multiple infirmities.

Hal "Boss" Peterson sat atop a giant South Texas business empire in the years before World War II. But despite his legendary business prowess, Boss was beset with a variety of physical ailments that limited his activities: heart disease, arthritis in his back and limbs which made moving about painful, emphysema which ravaged his lungs and reduced his breath, bad teeth, and a host of other more minor frailties. Any one of these maladies would have sidelined a less robust player.

After his first heart attack at age thirty-six, which resulted in a three-month hospital stay, the chain-smoking, hard-drinking Boss logged a significant portion of his life in hospitals.

One night in the late 1930s while talking with his physician, Dr. Leon Kopecky, Boss reflected about the need for a hospital in his hometown of Kerrville, a ranching town in the heart of the Hill Country. Boss, who had spent most of his hospital time in San Antonio, noted that Kerrville had only a "rattletrap hospital," Dr. Kopecky recalled.

"I want to do something for Kerrville," the doctor remembered Boss saying. And the two men realized in an instant what Boss's greatest vision would become: a state-of-the-art medical facility in the heart of the Texas hills.

True to his heritage as a bigger-than-life Lone Star entrepreneur, Boss didn't just want to build a hospital. His vision was to create the "Mayo Clinic of the South" along the banks of the sparkling clear Guadalupe River in Kerrville. Boss ran his idea past his brother, Charlie, and shared it with Guy Griggs, the business partner who served as Boss's lieutenant and chief executive officer. But the vision had to remain only in Boss's head during World War II.

As the end of the war came in sight in 1944, the Hal and Charlie Peterson Foundation was formed with a simple $100 contribution by Boss.

The two brothers committed their considerable resources to the new Foundation, which would have as its inaugural project a hospital that would cost three quarters of a million dollars. Construction of the downtown Kerrville hospital began in 1947 with the Foundation borrowing about half of the needed $750,000. The new fifty-five-bed, four-floor facility was dedicated and given to the people of the Texas Hill Country on July 3, 1949. The hospital was named Sid Peterson Memorial Hospital, in memory of Hal and Charlie's father. The plain-spoken dedication from Hal and Charlie reads:

> We have built this hospital as a memorial to our father. He grew up in the Hill Country, he loved it, and he counted his friends on Hill Country farms and ranches by the score. We think he would want us to erect this sort of memorial to him; a hospital that fills a need of long standing, dedicated without profit to the service of the community he loved.
>
> And so here it is; it's yours to use. If it will ease a little the sufferings of the sick and injured, if it will help a little to mend their broken bodies, if it will provide a place where the next generation—and the next—can enter this world with the best of care and attention, and if it can do these things at a minimum of expense to those who must be patients, then our purpose in building it and giving it to the Hill Country community has been well served. — Hal Peterson and Charlie Peterson.

In the early part of the twentieth century, before the national government was involved in health care, hospitals had to do much of the healing through charity, since many patients could not possibly pay. As a result, nobody really wanted to get into the hospital business. Doctors often were forced to set up their own hospitals if they were to have one in which to practice.

As medical technology began to expand the investment necessary to fund a modern hospital and keep up with scientific advances to save lives, taxpayers were increasingly called upon for financial support, normally through local government. In some cases, religious or charitable organizations underwrote the cost of these money-losing hospital ventures.

What motivated Hal and Charlie Peterson, the Hill Country masters of building businesses for profit, to create a Foundation to build a nonprofit hospital? According to associates, that oft-asked question can only be answered by considering several dynamics.

The existing general hospital in Kerrville, named Secor Hospital, was small and sub-par even by rural 1940s standards, and no one doubted that this growing city which was increasingly serving as the "Capital of the Texas Hill Country" needed an improved facility. Boss had the vision to see that a first-class hospital in the middle of ranching country would cement the city's claim as the area's premier town.

Hal and Charlie's father, Sid, died in a San Antonio hospital because the family felt there had been no suitable place to care for him in Kerrville. His death could have been another reason the brothers began to think about building a hospital for Kerrville.

One might think that Boss would want a hospital in Kerrville because of his many and varied illnesses and often prolonged hospital stays. But even though the Foundation's hospital had a Peterson Floor, and Charlie was a regular patient there, Boss apparently rarely stayed in the hospital. Associates can remember only one period of several weeks when Boss had several rooms on the top floor. By the time the hospital was completed in 1949, Boss had logged many stays in San Antonio hospitals. And San Antonio was where his main physician, Dr. Kopecky, practiced despite much "arm twisting" by Boss to persuade the doctor to move to Kerrville.

Friends relate that Boss was influenced to create the Foundation and hospital because many of the powerful people he admired and considered his peers in South Texas, such as Capt. Charles Schreiner, who was sometimes called the "Father of the Hill Country," were leaving their own monuments for their various communities.

Then there had been the creation of the "excess profits tax" during the war years. The tax had made it difficult for Boss and Charlie to hold on to the money they made from the Kerrville Bus Company and other ventures. George Delavan, who was later associated with Boss in the famed Castle Hills development in San Antonio, remembered hearing Boss tell of the shock of being in a 92 percent tax bracket. Boss complained loudly, he recalled, that those taxes left him with only $17,000 the first year the Kerrville Bus Company made a million dollars in corporate profit.

The Hal and Charlie Peterson Foundation proved a way to retain the ability to direct some of the wealth earned by the two brothers by putting it in one big pile and keeping it in the Texas Hill Country, which they loved so dearly.

And perhaps Boss and Charlie even had a sense of immortality. When the hospital was built, both men had reached middle age, and it was obvious that neither would father a child to carry on the Peterson name. The "child they never had" could have been the hospital, which was named to honor the father who had built the Peterson name as a ranching pioneer.

CHAPTER 2

Pioneer Spirit

THE TEXAS HILL COUNTRY is a geographical and geological anomaly rising up out of the endless prairie land.

To a pioneer heading west in frontier Texas, the coastal savanna slowly yielded to rolling terrain which was increasingly semi-arid with each turn of the wagon wheel. Then, suddenly, the pioneer came upon an uplift of land which carried him from a few hundred feet above sea level to up to 2,000 feet high amid rocky peaks, cedar trees, and free-flowing springs which quickly became pure blue rivers.

The pioneer who was sweating his way across the Lone Star State must have been uplifted along with the elevation as he wandered into what most Texans to this day consider something very close to heaven. Here were small mountains in a land famous for its flat, even terrain. Here were bountiful streams in a country noted for its dryness.

But if the pioneer kicked at the soil, he could quickly see it was not for farming. This was ranch country. The rocky nature of most Hill Country land has always favored the herder over the row-cropper. In many parts of the Hill Country, folks smile frequently at the absurdity of planting a $10 tree in a $500 hole which had to be blasted with dynamite.

The Texas Hill Country, a name which most Americans first

heard when Lyndon Johnson was president, stretches upward through the heart of Central Texas for an area that is about 200 miles square. Generally, the Hill Country is defined as being west of Austin and San Antonio but east of San Angelo, where the Great Southwestern Desert begins to form. While some rich soil exists along its river bottoms, the hills are better known for their pink granite and Austin stone. It is most certainly one of the best places to see the state-flower bluebonnet, the prickly pear, and the startling yellow explosions of flying pollen when the first blasts of winter erupt the mountain cedar trees.

The Hill Country became the line of a string of forts in the mid-nineteenth century which were formed to keep the Native Americans west of the settled land. The hills were beautiful but rugged.

Most of the people who migrated to the Texas Hill Country in the last half of the nineteenth century came to ranch. But the Peterson family originally came to Kerrville to farm and participate in the furniture business.

An entry in a family Bible reveals that Sidney Clay "Cap" Peterson was born in Lavaca County near the Texas coast on January 15, 1868. His middle name of "Clay" honored a distant cousin, the American patriot Henry Clay.

The Peterson family's roots ran back to the East Coast. William Caswell Peterson, Sidney's father and Hal and Charlie's grandfather, was born in Caswell County, North Carolina, in 1835. William was married to Lucy Ann Wright in Batesville, Mississippi. Lucy was a native of Perry County, Alabama, where she was born in 1836. William and Lucy had ten children.

Their first child, Elizabeth, was born in Mississippi. "Lizzie" married Benjamin Franklin Baker in 1881, and they had twelve children. She became "Aunt Lizzie" to many Peterson nieces and nephews. One son, Sidney Baker, would later serve in World War I and be buried in France. Sidney Baker's name now graces Kerrville's main north and south boulevard.

After his family had moved to Texas in 1862, William enlisted in the Confederate Army and was away from home for three long years (with one leave granted in 1863). He joined Company B, Cavalry Battalion, in Waul's Texas Legion, and served until May of 1865.

While in the army, William wrote "long and concerned letters" to his older brother, Sanders, who with his wife Elizabeth lived in Hallettsville in Lavaca County, where they looked after William's wife, Lucy, and her babies.

In a letter to his brother from the war, William captured the optimism of the Southern soldiers when he wrote:

> We are camped near Warrington 18 miles below Vicksburg. We can hear the roar of the cannon more or less daily though the main battle has not yet come off, but it is expected daily. Two of the Yankee gun boats passed down, and we captured them between Port Hudson and Vicksburg. The cry is peace—peace, and there is great disaffection in the federal army. They are as you see by the news deserting by thousands. Again in our favor. Three hundred thousand of their troops' time will be up in May, and the deserters and their own journals say they will not reenlist. Again, four of the northwestern states are going to hold a convention the fourth of March for the purpose of seceding and going with the Confederacy. The governors of those states have ordered in all of their troops. It is the prevailing opinion that we will be certain of peace this spring. This is all the news of any importance.

William went on to say: "This is badly rote, but I had to rite this on my knee, and you must excuse it."

William was later captured and held as a prisoner of war by the North. Following his release, William returned to Lavaca County. In the days when "carpetbaggers" ruled the South, the family knew the leanness of poverty and the necessity of hard work.

When Sid was two years old, father William moved the family further inland from Lavaca County to Gonzales County, some seventy miles east of San Antonio. A dozen years later, the family transplanted itself to Kerrville some seventy miles west of San Antonio, and the Peterson name came to the Hill Country to stay. William Peterson farmed and, for a few years, held an interest in Fawcett Furniture Store.

The Kerrville area had first been settled in the 1850s, when a small colony of adventurers came to the Hill Country with the idea of filling the need for building materials in San Antonio. At the time they arrived, the Hill Country was populated mostly by the German pioneers who began coming to the colony established by the German Immigration Company at New Braunfels. Many of these pioneers had pushed westward. The first settlement was made at

Fredericksburg some thirty miles north of Kerrville in 1846, and a community was established at Comfort, fifteen miles south of Kerrville, a few years later. The German families banded together into small towns for protection against Indians and outlaws.

The first Kerrville adventurers realized that shingles and logs from the immense cypress trees along the Guadalupe River would be profitable when carried down to the more populated and growing San Antonio area, which had a scarcity of building materials since it was mostly bushy mesquite country. The land on which the first shingle camp was established was owned by Joshua D. Brown, and the first settlement became known as Brownsborough. When the county was organized in 1856, Brown apparently pushed for the county to be named Kerr, in honor of his friend, the Texas pioneer James Kerr. Eventually, the town was named Kerrville.

For a number of years, the name of the town was often written "Kerrsville." Many German settlers called the town "Carrville." But in the late 1860s, when Capt. Charles Schreiner was county and district clerk, he dropped the superfluous "s," and the name became Kerrville.

It was shortly after 1880 when the Peterson family settled at their homestead farm three miles south of Kerrville near the spot where the veterans' hospital stands today (1999). The land was along the river bottom of the Guadalupe. Sid Peterson has been quoted as saying that he determined to be a rancher when he was a boy sitting on the rocks along the bank and watching that amazingly clear water churn past him.

William Peterson often spoke of the family's first Kerr County home, which had been constructed for protection against Indian attack. The small shed room had been built with cypress lumber and faced with rocks to keep Indian arrows from penetrating the walls, he said. The abundant arrowheads and beads found on the land indicated that the flat had long been a favorite campsite of Indian tribes.

The family history notes that Sid brought a "certain zest to the family from the first. He had the twinkle in his eye that made him resemble his father; yet the steady gaze and sharply appraising look of his mother. With a ready supply of humorous anecdotes that could always lighten up the mood of the most solemn occasion, he had a rare empathy with people of all types and was beloved by those in close contact with him who referred to him as Captain or just Cap. Though he relished a chance to drive a hard bargain, he could also be counted on to recognize the need to help out regardless of who it was."

Sid's father, William Peterson, retired from active farming in the year 1900, and he and his wife moved into Kerrville and lived on the corner of Barnett and Clay streets. William bought an interest in the furniture business of his son-in-law, W. A. Fawcett, in 1905, and William remained active in the business for a decade before age forced him to stay at home. He died in September of 1924, and his wife died nine months later.

Sid "Cap" Peterson was fourteen when the William Peterson family moved to Kerrville in 1882. He grew up as one of ten children, eight boys and two girls. The other sons were Leroy Clay, John, Walter, Thomas Black, Sanders, and Henry. One son, George Washington Peterson, died in infancy. The daughters were Elizabeth and Cornelia. Cornelia went on to marry W. A. Fawcett and linked the Petersons to another prominent Hill Country pioneer family. Cornelia's nickname came to be "Big Mama."

One of the brothers, Thomas Black Peterson, died from an accidental gunshot while duck hunting at Medina Lake. His death was the first tragedy to strike the Peterson family. Brother Walter Gray Peterson served as county tax assessor for two decades. Walter and his wife, Suzie Zula Philips, had four children: Zula Mae, Carl, Jack, and Annabel. All of Cap's brothers lived in Kerr County until their death.

Cap reportedly was fond of telling later in life how, as a boy, he loved to play in the live oak trees along the highway near Legion Hospital. A 1939 newspaper article quotes him as often joking that his education was limited to three months in the early-day schools. His poor eyesight is said to have prevented him from going beyond the grammar grades in elementary school; farming or stock raising seemed to be the only career option for Cap, according to an article in the *Pony Express Advertiser*.

Cap was a horse trader by nature. His sister, Cornelia Fawcett, told the story of a young Sid who exhibited the knack for trading. She recalled that he once gathered up bricks from a burned-out building and swapped them for a breeding sow. She said that even as a boy he knew that a trade without profit was a waste of effort.

The way young Sid saw it, the piglets the sow carried were "pure profit." Some versions of the story go that the youthful Sid eventually parlayed the litter of pigs into a spirited saddle horse.

Sid "Cap" Peterson learned the cattle business as a real cowboy, and while he was a young man, Cap joined two cattle drives up the famous old cattle trails to Kansas. When the coming of the railroads ended trail driving as an industry, Cap decided to settle down. The trail rides taught Cap to love horses and the outdoor life, and he concluded that the life of a rancher was his true calling, despite the problems with his heart that began to slow him prematurely.

At an early age, Cap exhibited a vision for the future. Instead of opposing the coming of the railroads as one might expect of a traildriver, stories relate that he was an early supporter of the railroad. Before the turn of the twentieth century, while Cap was fifteen years old and working as a $15-a-month "freighter," he heard talk about bringing a railroad into Kerrville from San Antonio. Cap offered to help—not with money because he had little, but with his back.

An early history of the Kerrville Bus Company relates that Sid "Cap" Peterson demonstrated his foresight and community spirit by struggling to help build a railroad so that Kerrville folks could have transportation to and from San Antonio. It is said that "Cap worked many hours on the first railroad into Kerrville and charged nothing for his time."

Cap married Myrta Goss, who was raised on the Goss farm fortuitously located adjacent to the Peterson homestead. Myrta Ellen (Goss) Peterson was born on February 15, 1881. To the end of his life, Cap called her "still the prettiest girl in seven counties" and always referred to her as Carrie. Soon the entire family called her Carrie. She proved a strong mother to their three sons. The couple began farming on the Goss farm east of Kerrville. The collective memory of Myrta is that she was "very much a lady" whose dignity was always visible, even when she was sitting. Myrta provided a solid Methodist upbringing for their sons.

One of the first natives of Kerr County, Myrta was the daughter of Spence Goss, the lone famed survivor of the Boneyard Indian Fight on the Divide area of the Hill Country west of Kerrville. As recorded by Clara Watkins in the Hill Country Preservation

Society's bicentennial edition of the history of Kerr County, the Spence Goss escape from Comanches has been retold countless times around Hill Country campfires and is "one of the gripping episodes of the winning of this country from the wilderness."

The history relates the incident as follows:

> Answering the call to go in pursuit of a marauding band of redskins in 1856, young Goss, Dan Murphy, and a Mr. Price encountered the Indians in what is now known as Boneyard Waterhole, in the western part of the county.
>
> In the ensuing battle, Murphy was slain. Although badly wounded, Price and Goss started the trip of about 45 miles back to the settlement. Price died on the way; but Goss continued the torturous journey alone, using a forked stick for a crutch. After 21 days of crawling over rocks, during which his only food was wild grapes and black haws which grew in the vicinity, the wounded man finally made his way to a shingle camp belonging to Doss Rees, near Sherman's Mill some 11 miles west of Kerrville.
>
> The return of Goss was hailed with great rejoicing throughout the settlement, for he had been given up as dead.
>
> Several years after this event, Mr. Goss joined the Confederate Army and was wounded in a clash with the Northern Forces on the Pedernales River.

Within this framework of frontier heritage, Sid "Cap" Peterson was raised, and he was married to the daughter of a Hill Country epic hero. Thus, the already big-framed man had little choice but to be bigger than life himself. Described as a character out of an Old West story, Cap had the self-reliant pride of a pioneer who knew no other way than to depend upon himself. He sometimes told how as a boy he walked behind the plow barefoot because he owned only one pair of shoes.

Nephew W. A. Fawcett recalled a story which revealed Sid's nature as follows:

> Someone wanted to sell Uncle Sid a Ford Ferguson tractor, and Uncle Sid said that if the tractor could plow as much ground in one day as Jehu (a black man who worked for Sid) could with four mules, he would buy it. By two or three o'clock in the afternoon, the tractor got a little ahead of Jehu. Uncle Sid warned Jehu that the tractor was going to beat him, but Jehu responded

> that he and his mules would "catch up in the cool of the evening, Cap." Jehu and the mules did beat the tractor, and Uncle Sid didn't buy it.

Cap continued to employ and support Jehu throughout his life. To repay his loyalty and service, Cap built the black man a small home in which to live as he aged.

A niece, Mrs. J. D. Patton, remembered that even when Sid Peterson was farming, the urge to ranch never left him. She said Sid told his family, "If you'll go to the ranch with me, I'll make you rich." Of course, she recalled, the family did go, and "everybody knows how successful he was."

Cap Peterson ranched at the Diamond Ranch in the rocky hills southwest of Kerrville near the town of Rocksprings, and at one time Hal and his father had ownership of some 60,000 acres under ranches called Diamond and Diamond Bar.

But ranching was a hard life full of financial peaks and valleys. Sid Peterson, like so many of the early Texas Hill Country ranchers and businessmen, benefited from the loyalty and persevering courage of the Schreiner family bank in Kerrville.

According to a story told by his nephew, Sid Peterson came into Kerrville in the early 1920s and told Louie Schreiner that he was going to have to "throw in the towel, that he just couldn't make it on the ranch." But Mister Louie handed Cap Peterson a checkbook and told him that the bank had been forced to repossess the Taylor Ranch, which was 12,600 acres between Rocksprings and Junction. Mister Louie told Cap to go back and run the Diamond Ranch and the Taylor Ranch too.

"If that's what you want me to do, I'll try it," Cap Peterson is reported to have replied. The attempt proved successful, with Cap eventually purchasing the Taylor Ranch from the bank for about $7 an acre. Most of Cap's relatively modest wealth reportedly came from land trading profits.

Mary Hyde Hutto remembered that her father, Lee Hyde, worked at the Diamond Ranch during one of the tight times. "Joe Sid and my father cut live oak for firewood and sold it by the cord. That's how hard times were," she said. "Every place that a Peterson bought they improved beautifully. That goes for Mister Sid and all three boys. They were great improvers of property."

An often-told story revealed what the name Sid Peterson meant in the Hill Country. When he needed to write a counter check for a large amount in a Rocksprings bank, the banker prudently telephoned Schreiner Bank in Kerrville to make certain the check would clear. But he was told by the Schreiner banker, "I don't care what the amount is. If Cap Peterson writes it, pay the draft."

One characteristic which marked Sid Peterson throughout his life was his love of a good horse. This was described in a publication released when the hospital was dedicated in his name:

> Whenever a stranger would ride by on a particularly fine animal, Cap would strike up a conversation, examine the horse, and, if possible, strike a bargain on the spot. He was a shrewd trader and drove a good bargain, but he never took advantage of the other fellow. And no one knew how long a horse would keep his fancy. As his sister, Mrs. W. A. Fawcett of Kerrville, expressed, it, "Sid would ride away on one horse in the morning and would ride back on another and still prettier one in the afternoon."

His sister also said the family knew when Cap was mulling over a cattle deal or a horse trade, because he would begin to whistle the sad and lonesome tunes of the cattle drives from Texas to Kansas. His sister said that whenever the family heard one of those tunes, the members knew to leave him alone. They knew Cap would not want to be disturbed while he was pondering the details of the deal.

Reportedly, Cap kept everything in his mind. It is said that although he concluded thousands of transactions involving cattle and horses, Cap never made so much as a single scratch on a piece of paper to record any of them. Reportedly, he could remember exactly what he paid for each animal, when he bought it, who he purchased it from, and to whom he sold it and for how much.

The eyesight problem which had ended his schooling was no match for the ability he had to keep facts and figures in his memory, his only ledger book. And this trait is one his son, Hal, would also display throughout his life.

But Cap had the Peterson heart problem, and he slowed down with age. Many people remember him sitting out in front of Peterson's Garage in his special place and talking to the world as it went past the heart of Kerrville. The employees of Peterson Interests called him "Cap'n Sid," and they told of his "almost uncanny ability to size up a workman." Whenever a new man came to a Peterson job, Cap would watch him and remark: "That fellow will do" or "That man is lazy." The employees said that Cap's first judgment would invariably prove correct.

His friends noted that Cap's ability to cut through social status was obvious in the way he played poker, a game the old horse trader loved. If he played with people who could afford it, he thought nothing about tossing $50 in the pot. But when he played with his less well-heeled friends, he would keep his bets to $2 or less.

Late in life when Cap had time on his hands and would hang around the auto company, he would play poker with the Peterson employees. He won so often that his sons cautioned him against "recapturing the Peterson wages."

Cap is said to have loved a joke on anybody, especially on himself. He loved to tell how someone had put the touch on him or gotten the best of him in any way.

Dr. Leon Kopecky, who treated both Cap and Boss, described Cap: "He was a great person, a wonderful personality. I can still hear him laughing. They say that he used to sit out in front of the auto garage whittling, which was fashionable at that time. He would bet on anything. If a furniture truck drove by, he would bet everybody 50 cents on where it was headed."

In the later years, Cap and Myrta left the homestead and moved into Kerrville on Earl Garrett Street for a few years, and they often enjoyed evenings at the home of the famed folk singer Jimmie Rodgers. But the call of the range took the couple back to the Diamond Ranch. Later, in the 1930s, Myrta's health made the move back into town imperative, and they occupied the house formerly owned by Rodgers, located at 617 W. Main in the Westland Addition, which Boss and Charlie had developed. The house had been called "the Blue Yodeler's Paradise" when Rodgers owned it. In September 1933, four months after Rodgers died, Hal engineered a deal, and Charlie Peterson bought the home for $5,250. At one time, Hal and Charlie shared the home with their parents, Cap and Carrie.

The family often lamented the fact that Cap would only stand still for a photograph if the picture also included one of his beloved horses. All of the pictures of Cap later in his life show him mounted very erect atop one of his steeds or holding the halter of one of his mares. This meant that few were closeups of Cap, and almost all captured him wearing his familiar gray business Stetson, which shadowed his eyes and covered most of his expression.

On September 8, 1939, after an illness of about ten days, Cap died in a San Antonio hospital from his heart ailment at age seventy-one. Cap was so well liked in the Texas Hill Country that his funeral was one of the area's biggest. People from all races and all economic strata traveled hundreds of miles to pay tribute.

An Austin newspaper described the scene in a Town Talk column:

> Several days ago, Sid C. Peterson of Kerrville died. When his funeral was held, hundreds of people thronged the yard, his home, to witness these last rites. It was about 57 years ago that Mr. Peterson moved to Kerrville from Gonzales. For 57 years, he had made his home in the Hill Country. For 57 years, he had worked, lived, and made friends in the Hill Country. And that was why so many people attended those last services.
>
> They called Mr. Peterson "Cap." He was interested mainly in ranching. He knew the ranch country. He knew the people. He loved the Hill Country, and he loved the people. He was the type who would walk down the street and it would sometimes take him an hour or so to get where he was going. That was because he liked to talk to people, and people liked to talk to him.
>
> Laborer or capitalist, he had a word with them. The sheep herder knew Mr. Peterson as well as the presidents of banks.
>
> He was a rugged pioneer Texas type, the individual who made his wealth from Texas but never lost the common touch. He had a true Texan's contempt for the ignorant, arrogant, get-rich-quickers. That was because many years before he had absorbed something from the Texas sunsets and rolling hills and purple twilights.

At his death, the *Kerrville Mountain Sun* wrote in tribute:

> The passing of Mr. Peterson severs a link connecting the beginning and the present. . . . He had not only witnessed during his spance the growth of the community from a frontier trading post to a city, but had himself played a vital part in this growth.
>
> His purse was always open to any enterprise which held the promise of adding to the importance of the city and county and

> to the betterment of its people. Hardly a subscription list had been circulated in the city in behalf of civic or charitable interests that has not had the name of Sid Peterson written near the top. He was that rare type of individual who sought neither limelight nor public honors for himself, and who labored constantly for the advancement of the county and community which he called his home.
>
> He was a man who was loved and respected by his fellow men. He typified the West, and on the streets after his passing, older men stood with tear-dimmed eyes and said, "He was a man who never went back on his word nor turned a deaf ear to a friend."
>
> Possibly his chief charm was his genuineness. . . . He was never stiff and formal. To those of his own age, he was "Sid." To the younger men and women, he was "Mister Sid" or "Uncle Sid." And with those whom he labored from day to day, he was their beloved "Captain."
>
> He was big of heart and stalwart of frame. . . . In the language of the range and cattle trail, "He was one to ride the river with."

The people who knew Cap Peterson remember the favorite expression he used for years. Cap would say, "Everything is 'copo-say,' " meaning that everything is all right. The term must have been Cap's version of "copacetic," which means that one is feeling tip-top, first-rate, excellent, fine.

The story goes that when Cap Peterson was in the hospital in San Antonio on September 8, 1939, he asked his nurse to adjust his pillow and fix his arms more comfortably. When she did it, Cap smiled up at her and said, "Now everything is copo-say." Those are believed to be his last words.

Chapter 3

Horse Trader Instinct

"Today, ranching is a bad habit," said Tom Syfan, who once raised Border collies for Hal Peterson, "but back then it was a good living."

In the early part of the twentieth century, the Sid "Cap" Peterson family was able to make a living ranching in the scenic but sometimes arid Texas Hill Country, despite economic downturns which apparently hit the family hard just before World War I and again in the early 1920s.

The Petersons were mostly cattle raisers, although much of the rugged Hill Country is more suited to raising goats. To this day, the Texas Hill Country remains one of the major producers of mohair in the world.

Cap's ranches were southwest of Kerrville, where people still remain the interlopers among the coyotes, deer, jackrabbits, wild turkey, and mountain lions. This vast expanse of ranching country is perhaps even less settled than it was in the first half of the century, when more rural families still tried to make their living solely from the land. The land's main cash value today comes from selling lucrative hunting leases to big city executives who are drawn to the eternally pristine hills a few weekends a year.

The Cap Peterson family ranch was not a corporate tax write-off. Cap fed his family by raising and selling cattle, a process that was not likely to make a family wealthy unless oil happened to lurk beneath the rocky surface. But the Hill Country is one of the rare regions in Texas where petroleum has not been discovered in abundance.

By all accounts, Cap made more of the family's money by "trading," especially in buying and selling land, than he did by raising cattle. By nature, he was a gambler, and he drew stimulation and sustenance from the art of the deal. For all of his love of horses and the ranching life, there were clear elements of the businessman in Cap. He is mostly pictured, not in the Stetson cowboy hat of the West, but in a felt fedora more commonly worn in town.

In this ranching and trading environment, Sid and Myrta Peterson raised their three boys. Hal was the first son born, on February 28, 1899. Two years later came Charlie Vann Peterson, on September 15, 1901. The youngest was Joe Sid Peterson, born another two years later, on October 28, 1903. During the rough rides across rock-strewn Hill Country roads, Cap liked to have his boys crawl out on the hood of the car to "toughen them up."

From childhood, the three boys were quite distinct in nature's strange way of shuffling the parental genes to deal each offspring a different hand to play. Hal apparently came out of the womb with a personality that might today be labeled "Type A." According to cousin Dash Peterson, the family has no recollection of the young Hal playing with toys. "He was born a man," Dash said.

Charlie proved most like his mother: quiet, soft, disciplined. He collected orphan animals and brought them home. And Joe Sid displayed his happy-go-lucky streak from boyhood.

Hal was most like his father, and the family often said, "Like father, like son." Hal was a "serious kid" who seemed to take to business instead of playing.

Perhaps Hal's nature is best revealed by his nickname of "Boss." Cap Peterson began calling his oldest son "Boss" when the boy was only about six years old, and the moniker fit so well that it stuck for a lifetime. Hal was always "Boss" to his family, his friends, his employees, his business associates, and even to the people in Kerrville who had never met him.

Boss picked up a number of attributes from his father. Like Mister Sid, Boss loved animals, especially horses, but unlike his father, as an adult Boss didn't ride.

When it came to cars, both father and son were basically riders. Mister Sid always had a driver for his T-model touring cars, and few people can ever remember seeing Boss behind a steering wheel.

But Boss often told childhood stories of how he and his brothers delivered horses for Cap. "When his dad would trade horses with someone, it might be twenty miles away," said a business associate. "Boss, Joe Sid, and Charlie would drive the horses over to deliver them. Boss said he rode many a mile on horseback delivering horses for his dad. He was very fond of his mother and dad . . . especially his dad."

As his father loved to do, Boss liked to "figure the angles" of any proposition. Even as a youth, he proved a natural "horse trader," as that type of Texan was called at the time. He had his father's successful gambler instinct for the statistically prudent risk.

While Cap had a strong and wide frame well over six feet tall, son Boss was shorter at about five feet, ten inches, and tended to be stouter, thicker, and more rotund. Boss grew to weigh more than 200 pounds, which didn't help the health problems that plagued him throughout his life. Hal had a round businessman's face which was pleasant but not handsome. His hairline quickly receded far up on his forehead, probably only enhancing his "thinking man" image.

On the other hand, second son Charlie had his mother's striking good looks. With boyish charm which lasted until his death, Charlie also stood about five feet, ten inches tall, but weighed only about 155 pounds.

If people were attracted to Boss's aura of power, women found Charlie's natural charm even more irresistible. Joe Sid had his father's height and the more gangly frame often associated with the working rancher. Something about Joe Sid was wild and untamed like the land he remained on all his life. If looks can be said to play any part in a person's destiny, then the three brothers looked their futures.

The Sid Peterson family did not endure the extremely remote life that many Texas ranching families were forced to live. Except for a period of hard times in the 1920s, when the family went back to the ranch, the family lived much closer to town than Cap's distant ranches.

His oldest son fit into the world of business as if he had been custom-made for the role. By the time he was a teenager, Hal (Boss) already had a bank account, and his checks were honored anywhere in the region. He was a child who earned his own money for fireworks at a time when most boys had to beg their fathers for the cash.

At the age of fifteen, Boss left the world of farming and ranching and set up business in town. At age sixteen, he began working at the M. F. Weston Garage, which was located at the intersection of Water Street and what is now Sidney Baker Street, an intersection above the north bank of the Guadalupe River which is still the heart of downtown Kerrville. He had a desk in the back corner where he would conduct small business ventures out of the top drawer. By age eighteen he owned the garage.

Boss's purchase of the Weston Garage, which became Peterson's Garage and Auto Company, signaled the official launching of Peterson Interests.

The business relationship that Boss had with his father is still unclear to this day. Boss was far too young to have established credit for the building of a business empire, and the name of his well-known and well-respected father was valuable currency. Early publications describe Sid "Cap" Peterson as the auto dealer and transportation owner, but those who remember say the young Boss was the driving force behind the businesses. In the last decade of his life, the father seemed to have an up-front position in times of ceremony but left most of the decision-making to his sons and their associates.

No matter how the ownership split out on paper, the Petersons appeared to consider business a family matter. The boys always deferred, at least in news stories on public occasions, to the father until his death in 1939. And the family tradition continued as Boss and Charlie remained equal partners throughout their lives, even though Boss clearly did almost all of the business work.

Possibly because Cap's eyesight problems had ended his education in early grammar school, the father always encouraged his sons' education. Boss went to school in Kerrville, then on to San Antonio Academy. Charlie also went to San Antonio Academy.

Boss entered the University of Texas but grew impatient with the slow pace of higher learning when he knew he could be out making money. After a year at the university, he transferred to

Eastman Business College in Poughkeepsie, New York, where he could concentrate on his business training. This was the same college which had trained banker Louis Schreiner. But Boss didn't remain long in the East. He soon returned to Kerrville to set his entrepreneurial spirit free.

The story is told that, as his boys came of age, Cap Peterson gave each of them money to launch business careers. Boss and Charlie pooled their money and went into transportation. Joe Sid invested his money in the Manhattan Cafe. The cafe went broke, and Joe Sid returned to the family ranch never to be involved in his two brothers' joint enterprises. By all accounts, the brothers remained close, but Joe Sid chose one path for his life, while Boss and Charlie went down another.

Hal and Charlie Peterson's grandparents, (left to right) Lucy Ann and William Caswell Peterson.

Above: *The "Jimmie Rodgers house" purchased by Hal Peterson for his parents, Mr. and Mrs. Sid Peterson, in Kerrville, Texas.*
— Photo courtesy of Dr. Rector

Below: *Singer Jimmie Rodgers, friend of Hal and Charlie Peterson, stands next to his automobile.*
— Photo courtesy of Starr Bryden collection

Photo taken for the newspaper at a stockholders' meeting for a new "nutcracker" gadget. Hal "Boss" Peterson is seated at the table between two women (sitting in profile). He is the fourth person from the right.

— Photo courtesy of the Starr Bryden collection

Water Street in downtown Kerrville during the 1930s. An early view of Peterson's Garage is visible at right.

— Photo courtesy of the Starr Bryden collection

Part Two

The Empire

Above: *A driving business of Peterson Interests—Peterson's Garage, formerly located at the corner of Sidney Baker and Water Street in downtown Kerrville, Texas.*

— Photo courtesy of Dr. Rector

Below: *Kerrville buses parked in front of Peterson's Garage. Drivers are Bill Jonas (left) and Gay Munn.*

— Photo courtesy of Kerrville Bus Company

CHAPTER 4

The Road to Success

THE HARDY FOLKS WHO pioneered the western part of Texas never took transportation lightly.

With its relatively sparse and spread-out population, West Texas seems almost as vast as the Australian outback. And like the outback Australians who consider a station (ranch) 200 miles away as a close neighbor, West Texans have grown accustomed to dealing with distance. A rancher and his wife think little of driving an hour or even two hours to reach a restaurant for dinner and then driving back later that night—a five- or six-hour trip that would cross three states in some portions of the U.S.

In the early part of the twentieth century, the Texas Hill Country must have appeared as vast and nearly as remote as the most distant regions in the West. When the only way to reach the small settlements which passed for Hill Country towns was a rocky, creek-bottom wagon ride, getting to a farm or ranch only a few miles from town was a hard day's trip. And a ranch thirty miles away as the crow flies forced its owners into rare pilgrimages to town for supplies, doctors, and other human interactions.

With that in mind, it is not so strange that the ranching Peterson family took an interest in transportation. After all, Cap Peterson in his youth had endured the most arduous compensation for lack of transportation when he joined trail rides which drove cattle from

South Texas far up to the railroad lines in Kansas. No one who had made that trip could ever in his lifetime overlook the importance of getting from point A to point B. No wonder he worked many hours for free to help bring the first railroad line into Kerrville.

The heart problems which afflicted Cap and later his sons also caused them to understand the importance of being able to reach a well-equipped San Antonio hospital as quickly as possible.

When the fifteen-year-old Boss Peterson "went to town" to launch his business career, he put his desk in a corner of the Weston Garage, one of the first of the businesses which would grow exponentially along with the automobile. It is said the youthful Boss recognized quickly the tremendous business potential the mechanized wagon would have in the far-flung Texas Hill Country. The seventy-mile trip to San Antonio could take days by wagon or horseback, but it could be a day trip with the assistance of an automobile.

In the World War I era, Cap Peterson owned many sections of land but not much more. The family was what the agrarian community calls "land poor." The Petersons had a good net worth if they sold their land, but not much cash otherwise, since ranching has always been more capital gain than cash flow.

By the time he was eighteen years old, Boss had purchased Weston Garage, although on paper the purchase was probably made by father Sid "Cap" Peterson. Early reports do not mention the family's second son, Charlie, as a member of this business deal, but Charlie came into the enterprise shortly thereafter. All subsequent deals were made by both Hal and Charlie.

Owning a garage in downtown Kerrville in the days before there were all that many automobiles enabled Boss to see the need to establish for-hire transportation, and soon the garage had cars taking ranchers to Rocksprings, Medina, Bandera, Comfort, Fredericksburg, Junction, and the many other communities, ranches, and farms that were coming alive in the Texas hills.

The formal start of the Petersons' business interests was delayed until the mid-1920s, probably for a number of reasons. Hal and Charlie were young and needed some education and seasoning. The early part of the decade proved an economically difficult time for the family, and the Petersons retreated to the ranch to weather the four years of hard times.

Although the father advised and lent his considerable standing to the in-town business, it was clearly Boss who had the vision of what the garage could eventually be. Soon his three sedans were making regular daily runs between Kerrville and San Antonio. It was a bus company long before it was called a bus company. At first, people rode in whatever vehicle the garage had on hand, but Boss soon purchased stretched Buicks to carry more passengers. The Buicks could hold six to eight passengers. In 1924 Boss officially launched the Kerrville Bus Company as a partnership with his brother, Charlie.

A booklet entitled *The Story of the Kerrville Bus Company* described the early business this way:

> In 1926, Calvin Coolidge was serving his second term as president. A loaf of bread cost five cents. A pound of coffee was 30 cents. Charlie Chaplin was in his prime. . . . In Kerrville, Texas, rancher Sid Peterson had also become an automobile dealer and along with this business was using three sedan cars to take people to San Antonio to shop, to the hospital, or to get transportation to other parts of the country. Sid's two sons, Hal and Charlie, were helping with this new venture. . . .
>
> The railroads had fallen on hard times, and the people in the Hill Country were delighted with the new service. Those were the days when many families did not even own one car. Kerrville had no hospital and very few shops. The drivers would shop for Kerrville ladies if they would send along a sample of material or thread. Upon his return, the driver would make his delivery, and whatever he collected was his. And so was born Package Express.

Officially written company histories place the father in the foreground. These histories say the father received help from his sons, but those who remember say Boss was the boss—with helpful advice from the well-respected Sid Peterson. What role Charlie played in the early company is unclear, but Boss probably needed Charlie, not only for the contribution of his investment money provided by Cap to all his sons to begin their business careers, but also for the stability that Charlie possessed to help rein in his more volatile and impulsive older brother.

One irony of the Peterson transportation business is that the man who made a fortune with a company who drove people from place to place did not drive himself. Boss, like his father Cap, always had someone else behind the wheel.

By 1925, Boss formally turned the garage, which was located in the heart of downtown Kerrville, into Peterson's Garage and Auto Company. From the outset, Boss believed in General Motors, and his hunch proved a good one. His first franchise to sell automobiles was Buick from General Motors. Then he acquired Chevrolet, Oldsmobile, Pontiac, and Cadillac, in that order, becoming one of the few dealerships in the nation to have all of the General Motors products under one roof.

Once again, Boss did not form Peterson's Garage and Auto Company on his own. (The name of the company eventually was changed to indicate a plural ownership, as Petersons'.) By the time the auto company officially organized, it was understood that Charlie was an equal partner. Even in the early days, however, Charlie never came to the office very much, except to endure the meetings Boss insisted upon calling.

The old-timers who recall the young Boss remember that he was a student of how men acquired great wealth in America, particularly John D. Rockefeller, who had built Standard Oil into the largest empire in the early part of the century. Boss noted that Rockefeller had accomplished this by controlling the oil industry at all levels, from drilling to processing to distribution to sales at the pump.

An original and abstract thinker, Boss decided he would try to build the same kind of linearly integrated company in transportation. He deliberately tried to get in the business at all levels, an ambitious—and, many thought, foolhardy—undertaking for two young brothers isolated far out in the Hill Country. Although far less successful than Rockefeller, Boss still managed to make the concept work Texas-style.

Boss also had interest in a company called American Pure Milk. When the Legion Hospital was moved from Houston to Kerr County, the colonel in charge of the hospital told Boss that it was unfortunate no creamery in Kerrville was available to supply milk, butter, and cream to the hospital. Boss filled the gap by founding the American Creamery, later named American Pure Milk. The Peterson farm near Legion Hospital served as the first dairy for the creamery, which was sold a few years later to Boss's cousins, two brothers named Carl and Jack Peterson. Often called "the creamery," the milk distributor was eventually located near Five Points in Kerrville.

The Texas Legislature had moved to regulate the transportation business by passing the Motor Bus Act, also called the Beck Bus Law, in 1927. The state awarded nine temporary certificates to operate between San Antonio and Kerrville. Five went to J. C. Power and one to Joe Amberson (Union Bus Company), who were also operating "stage" lines between the two cities.

A book entitled *Intercity Bus Lines of the Southwest: A Photographic History* by Jack Rhodes relates the historical importance of the regulatory battle involving the early Kerrville Bus Company in this way:

> One of the major independent companies to emerge and survive during the late twenties was the Kerrville Bus Company, an efficient, well-managed intercity bus line which still provides service throughout much of Texas. The history of this company is of special interest because it includes the first full-scale dispute adjudicated by the Railroad Commission involving making permanent the temporary certificates and permits issued under the grandfather clause of 1927.
>
> At the time of regulation a triumvirate of bus lines plied between San Antonio and Kerrville, all operating converted automobiles. The Railroad Commission had granted temporary permits to J. L. and J. A. Power for five and a half trips per day, to Hal Peterson for two and a half trips daily, and to Union Bus Company for two additional round trips daily.
>
> In the summer of 1927, all three permit holders filed for permanent certificates, with Union Bus Company protesting any permanent rights for the Power and Peterson families, and the Powers and Hal Peterson protesting any awarding of certificates to the Union Bus Company.
>
> Because the hearing involved the first major dispute of franchise rights under the Beck Bus Law, the Railroad Commission took extensive testimony, consolidated the three applications into a single case, and staged the first hearing at Kerrville on August 26, 1927. Another hearing convened in Austin on August 28, and the final session occurred in Kerrville on October 1, 1927.
>
> During the course of the hearings, evidence was introduced to show that J. L. Power had begun service between Kerrville and San Antonio in August of 1921. By 1925 the Union Bus Com-

pany had added service of its own, and also in 1925, Hal Peterson had purchased two Buick sedans and had begun service over the same route. A mutual agreement had been reached that stabilized the service at ten round-trips a day, divided as indicated among the Power family, Hal Peterson, and the Union Bus Company.

During the hearings the Union Bus Company contended that Peterson and Power were actually operating as its agents while driving their schedules, that they had used the Union Terminal in San Antonio, displayed the Union Bus Company flag on their vehicles, paid a charge of one dollar per departure from the San Antonio terminal, and otherwise acted as subsidiary operators for the company. Union Bus Company contended that it alone was therefore the owner of the franchises.

Peterson and Power saw their relationship with Union to be quite different from the interpretation placed on it by the company. They acknowledged the fees paid to Union and the use of the company flag and terminal facilities, but stated that they had retained separate identities primarily because they, not the Union Bus Company, were liable for damages to passengers or property incurred on their runs. They also pointed to Union's two separate schedules per day as *prima facie* evidence that a distinction existed between their operations and those of the company.

On December 3, 1927, the commission held that J. L. and J. A. Power and Hal Peterson had operated their schedules in good faith prior to January 11, 1927, not as agents of the Union Bus Company but as private independent operators. The ruling stipulated that Union be given permanent certificates between San Antonio and Kerrville for only two daily round-trips, not the ten the company sought, and that the Powers and Peterson should divide the other eight so that half runs would be eliminated. In other words, the commission found that, although the Union Bus Company has performed a commendable and useful service to the public in furnishing a central place for the arrival and departure of motor passenger vehicles, this service did not entitle the company to absolute permanent rights that would harm the independent operators who had used the company's facilities.

Kerrville Bus Company began to move toward incorporation and expansion in December of 1928, not long before the start of the Great Depression in 1929. In that year of the great stock market crash, Boss saw opportunity. While the entire nation was in turmoil and in retreat, Boss purchased the operating certificates of the Union Bus Company (Amberson) as well as the Power interests, and soon Kerrville Bus Company controlled all the bus service in the Hill Country.

In 1929 the road from San Antonio was paved out nineteen miles toward Kerrville. In those days the road was dirt through hills and valleys until it reached within eight miles of Kerrville, where the pavement began again. Provided weather conditions were perfect, the vehicles of Kerrville Bus Company could make the run in two and a half hours, significantly more than twice the time required along Interstate 10 today. The thousands of springs in the Hill Country created creeks and rivers which meant the company's Buicks had to traverse numerous low water crossings, and many times they were unable to do so. Any rainfall which caused the rivers to swell severed the Hill Country from San Antonio.

The rural intercity bus business proved as tough an enterprise as Hill Country ranching, and only determined, efficient operators survived.

CHAPTER 5

"Looking After" the Business

A VISIONARY OFTEN HAS the problem of myopia.

Hal "Boss" Peterson always looked far down the road to the horizon. But what kept him from tripping over the potholes beneath his feet?

Early in his business career, Boss developed a style of operation which mostly served him well and only occasionally brought him ill. To keep his eyes on the horizon, Boss sought out trusted and talented lieutenants to make sure he avoided the potholes.

In those days, they called it "looking after" the business. Boss had someone "looking after" Peterson's Garage and Auto Company. Boss had someone "looking after" Kerrville Bus Company. In this sense, Boss exhibited the instincts of today's best entrepreneurial investors who always make certain they have the right operator in place to mind the business before risking their money.

By the time Kerrville Bus Company had formed, Boss had found an exceptional lieutenant to look after the growing Peterson Interests. This lieutenant was Guy Griggs, a native of Hillsboro, Texas. Griggs, as so many families had done, moved to the Texas Hill Country in 1924 because he had tuberculosis. Giving up a job in a Beaumont retail store, The White House, Griggs was twenty-eight years old when he arrived at Kerrville for treatment at the tuberculosis clinic and sanitarium operated by Dr. Sam Thompson.

Willa Mae Gibson recalls Griggs telling the story that on arrival he was "dead broke and hoping for a miracle." While staying at the sanitarium, Griggs worked for Dr. Thompson to pay for his room and board.

Folk singer Jimmie Rodgers was perhaps the most famous Kerrville tuberculosis patient. Many suffering families joined the wagon yard at what the locals called the "TB Colony." Tuberculosis brought many of today's prominent families to the Texas Hill Country in search of Kerrville's higher, drier air which doctors recommended in the early part of the century. This caused tuberculosis camps to dot the banks of the Guadalupe River. Many who expected to die found themselves getting better and remained in the Hill Country for life.

Even though his case of tuberculosis was officially listed as "arrested," Griggs always took a nap after lunch to keep from getting tired, which might allow the disease to come back. When Griggs married in his late thirties, his wife, Edna Mae, was cautioned against marrying Griggs because he had suffered with TB and was almost twenty years older than she was. Griggs, however, proved the skeptics wrong and lived to be eighty-two.

Guy Griggs went to work for Kerrville Bus Company in 1926 and was secretary at its incorporation in 1929. He progressively moved up to general manager, then to vice president and general manager, then to president, and finally to chairman of the board in 1963. When he died on November 30, 1980, he had spent fifty-four years working with Peterson Interests, including overseeing the management of the hospital as secretary-treasurer-manager of the Hal and Charlie Peterson Foundation. Although never to his face, close business associates affectionately referred to him as "Papa Griggs," a nickname still heard in Kerrville conversation.

When the newly incorporated Kerrville Bus Company held the election of its board of directors on January 8, 1930, Griggs was the first non-family member to appear as an officer on the board. The officers were:

Hal Peterson	*President*
Sid Peterson	*Vice President*
Guy G. Griggs	*Secretary*
Charlie Peterson	*Treasurer*

According to the company history, the board instructed Secretary Griggs to notify the local newspapers that there was now a new corporation: Kerrville Bus Company, Inc.

Although he was a tall Texan, the six-foot, five-inch Griggs did not have the kind of personality that felt compelled to stand out in a crowd. He left that to Boss.

Griggs was the detail man who tended the financial statements and handled the cash flow. He lived a quiet life, especially compared to the excitement which constantly swirled around Boss. Kerrville attorney Joe Burkett described it this way: "Guy Griggs was a brilliant man. He was firm in his opinion and had no hesitancy to tell Boss what he thought. He was one of the most capable businessmen and honorable citizens in this area. Boss had the good judgment to employ Griggs and trust him. One of the great strengths of Boss was in his selection of people. Boss only dealt with people who knew what they were doing."

With the purchase of the Winn Way Stage Company in late 1930, Kerrville Bus operated routes from Austin to Houston and from Austin to Lampasas. The company history reports that Kerrville Bus had acquired a variety of vehicles in many sizes and vintages. The company rebuilt many of them and purchased three new GMC 21-passenger coaches with hard-to-obtain 1930s credit.

The history notes:

> As Kerrville Bus Company enlarged, so did its payroll. It was necessary to have more drivers, garage space and mechanics as well as a larger office force. The automobile dealership building was a busy place . . . the offices for the dealership and the Bus Company were all together, and you could not tell where one ended and the other one began. By 1931, the company began to realize that prosperity was not just around the corner, and if it was to survive, the company was going to have a bus that was more economical to operate, and the payroll would have to be reduced. They started using used parts and haunted the used parts lots. Fortunately, they could find Buick parts. Schedules were adjusted to eliminate a run here and there. Employees took cuts in wages to allow the barest of a living. Some management men worked without pay and drew just enough money for an existence.

With a desperate need to reduce costs and with his vision of a vertically integrated company in his head, Boss began to look for a cheaper way to obtain his buses. In those depression days, most manufacturing companies had gone out of business, and the remaining ones expressed reservations about helping a regional independent company. But Boss persisted, and the corporate minutes of Kerrville Bus Company describe the result:

> On one of his trips to the East, Mr. Peterson ran into C. D. Beck, who had some previous bus body building experience. Mr. Beck was looking for something to do, and Mr. Peterson contacted a Mr. Cummins, president of a Sidney, Ohio, bank. The Anderson Body Company of Sidney, Ohio, had closed down, and the bank owned the building and equipment that had previously been owned by Anderson. After negotiations, a partnership was worked out whereby Mr. Cummins put up the building and equipment, Mr. Beck put up his experience and "know how" and Mr. Peterson put up enough working capital to start the operation. This was the beginning of C. D. Beck and Company. (The Peterson Interests owned one-third of the Beck Bus Company, while Beck owned a third, and Ohio and Texas banks shared ownership in the remaining third.)
>
> Kerrville Bus Company obligated itself to buy the first bus built by the new company; this bus was driven to Texas by C. D. Beck himself. In fact, that was the practice followed for some time. The factory would complete a bus, and if it were not already sold, C. D. Beck would take the bus on the road and sell it while another one was being constructed.
>
> The first bus was an eleven passenger body mounted on a modified Chevrolet truck chassis. This was not the most stylish or comfortable means of travel, but it was cheap to operate and went a long way towards the ability of Kerrville Bus Company to continue in business.
>
> The capacity of the bus was soon increased to sixteen passenger size and eventually to twenty-one passenger size. The bus was, of course, improved in appearance and comfort as time went by and became very popular throughout the industry. As the depression eased, an International truck chassis was used with modification, and the size of the bus increased.

In what was great foresight for those days, Boss figured that the bus company could purchase a bus, drive it for several years, then drive it down into Mexico and sell it for close to the original cost.

Griggs had been running the Austin office for Kerrville Bus Company when Boss called him back to Kerrville to "look after" the whole bus company and eventually the entire Peterson Interests. When Griggs returned, he asked Willa Mae (Braden) Gibson to be his secretary. Willa Mae began working in the garage and auto company office. This proved to be a perfect business team; Willa Mae served as Griggs's assistant for forty-two years and held every office position in the company, including assistant secretary to the board of directors, which was an unusually high position for a woman at the time. For decades, Willa Mae was the spoke around which the wheel of Peterson Interests revolved.

Willa Mae said that when Boss came into the office, it was "strictly business." She never made any personal appointments for him. She was secretary for both Boss and Griggs, but she worked much more closely with Guy Griggs.

"Boss had too many interests. He was a start-up person. Details were not his business. Boss got the ideas, and then he pitched them into Mr. Griggs's lap. . . . Mr. Griggs was a true business executive, very professional. . . . He was interested in the bottom line," said Willa Mae, who retired in 1976.

"One thing about the Kerrville Bus Company is that it tried to keep new buses. As soon as the buses got old, they were sold to bus companies in Mexico. It was a big business reselling the old buses . . . and profitable too. Schreiner Bank financed the sale of the buses to Mexican companies, which was quite a concession since there was no way to collect if they didn't pay. But they paid like clockwork. We never lost a dime on one of those buses," Willa Mae said.

When many businesses were sinking in the Great Depression, Boss and his associates paddled and bailed and managed to keep his fledgling companies afloat. He obtained the rights to operate between Kerrville and Junction in 1929, from Austin to Houston and Lampasas in 1930, from Austin to Kerrville in 1933, and from Austin to Victoria in 1936.

Although Kerrville Bus Company remained independent, the firm built an alliance with Greyhound which served it well. Kerrville Bus was able to operate from Greyhound terminals in San Antonio, Houston, and Austin, and leased some far West Texas routes around Pecos from Greyhound until after World War II. The company prospered with J. D. Mahaffey "looking after" the bus company as its president.

With the company expanding and the depression easing, times for the Petersons were poised to leap from hard to good—very, very good.

CHAPTER 6

Personal Glimpses

HAL "BOSS" PETERSON did not possess what women might call handsome looks. His face and his body were a bit too rotund, his eyebrows a little too thick, his hairline slightly receding to leave a tad too much forehead.

But even at an early age, Boss had the attraction of self-confidence and the aphrodisiac of power all about him.

And he was a man who leapt into action the moment he made a decision, according to Charles Johnston, a Kerrville native who for decades managed Peterson's Garage and Auto Company for Peterson Interests. Johnston was in the room and, because it was such unusual action, clearly remembers one of the watershed moments in Boss's life.

Boss and Dora Katherine Johnston had been high school sweethearts. Dora was born in the year 1900, making her one year younger than Boss. The two might have been married following school, but succumbing to that strange genetic attraction which often draws young women to the mystery of the stranger, Dora ran off with a salesman from South Dakota. The couple had a daughter, named Kathleen.

The marriage did not work, and soon Dora was back in Kerrville, a divorced woman with a young daughter. In the 1920s divorce carried a stigma which might have kept most young men from one of the town's most prominent families away, but not Boss. Soon Boss had forgiven Dora and was seeing her again.

One evening, Boss was visiting Dora at the Johnston family residence located on Water Street, where the One Schreiner Center office building is now (1999). The two were sitting in the living room with Dora's young nephew, Charles Johnston, who was playing nearby. Charles remembers Boss suddenly and quite impulsively saying: "Let's get married. Call the preacher."

They did, and the two were married that night, on July 29, 1927, in the Johnstons' living room.

By all accounts, Boss truly adored Dora, and he loved and treated her daughter as he would his own child. The life Boss lived might have been much personally happier and even much longer had Dora and Kathleen survived. In 1933, Kathleen died of leukemia at age twelve. Charles Johnston recalled his parents discussing "those tough years when both Boss and Dora were devastated by Kathleen's death." More grief would come three years later when Dora died, at the age of thirty-six, while on a fishing trip with Boss in Corpus Christi. She choked on a fish bone. Her senseless death sent Boss into a personal depression that lasted many years but did not diminish his determination to grow Peterson Interests.

Frank Stanush, a business associate, said, "Boss had adopted Kathleen, and he was crazy about her. I was with Boss many times when he told how he cried like a baby over losing them."

Boss remained a widower until 1947, when he impulsively married a striking woman named Audrey Ralls, described by some of the women in Kerrville as a "grass widow" who was divorced from her husband but not really a widow. The fiery Romeo and Juliet courtship between Boss and Audrey "raised eyebrows in town."

Boss had known Audrey for a number of years after having met her at Beverly Studios. Later, Audrey became a public relations person for Southern Select Beer in Houston, according to Dr. Kopecky. "She could sing, and play a piano. She was a marvelous piano player. They were married in the Menger Hotel in San Antonio, and there were only eight or ten people there," said Kopecky, who attended with his wife.

Stanush said Boss and Audrey "got along great until they got married." Boss later said that he hadn't been married but a few minutes before he knew this marriage was not made in heaven. After a brief seventeen months without marital bliss, Boss and Audrey had the most friendly of divorces, and Audrey walked away with a large sum of money. At the moment when the divorce settlement was signed and the two were officially unjoined, Boss dropped down on his knees at Audrey's feet and looked up at her.

"I've always wanted to marry a wealthy woman," Boss joked to his new ex-wife. "Audrey, would you marry me?"

Except for the very brief marriage to Audrey, Boss lived the single life from the time Dora died until 1954, when he married the woman who was to be his companion for the remainder of his life.

Billie Ligon O'Daniel remembered the first time she saw the legendary Boss Peterson crossing the street with two other men in front of Pampell's Drug Store in downtown Kerrville. This was during the 1930s, when Billie and her husband Edgar "Fats" Fatheree owned the Fatheree Funeral Home on the corner of Sidney Baker and Water Street across from Peterson's Garage.

Boss had stopped and bought Billie's daughter, Betty Lee, the young girl's very first ice cream cone.

"Boss was a wonderful person," Billie said, "but you didn't just like him right away. He was a generous man but not a public man. He didn't want any of the credit."

As a young single woman, Billie Ligon had graduated as valedictorian of her nursing school at Physicians and Surgeons Hospital in San Antonio. "From that day on," said Betty Lee about her mother, "she never wanted to be anything else. Actually she was a nurse all her life whether she was employed or not. She was a caregiver, always concerned about her family's comfort and welfare and that extended to all of her friends. That was the way mother lived her life, by taking care of people and making sure they were happy."

In the late 1930s, Billie and her husband "Fats" closed their Kerrville Funeral Home and moved with Betty Lee to San Antonio, where Billie went to work at the Nix Hospital. While at the Nix, it is very possible that Billie nursed Boss and Cap Peterson during their hospital stays. In 1946 the Fatherees moved to Dallas. Shortly after the move, Billie's husband died.

"Mother stayed in Dallas until Boss called her in the early '50s," said Betty Lee. "There may have been a gap in their communication over the years, but there was never a gap in the friendship."

Betty Lee was attending Baylor University during the time that Boss and Billie began seeing each other, and Billie was "scared to death" her daughter wouldn't like Boss. Billie and Boss met Betty Lee at the bus station. Boss went over and put his hand on his future stepdaughter's shoulder, and Betty Lee said, "We have come a long way, Boss, since that first ice cream cone."

She described her relationship with Boss:

"Boss wanted very much to be fatherly. He was very solicitous of me, maybe a little awkward at first because I think that it was obvious by that time that he wanted to marry my mother.

"I remember one time he had just put a pool in the backyard at his home on 101 Morningside in San Antonio. The concrete was barely dry, and it was still empty. When I came home from school that weekend, Boss talked the fire department into filling the pool with water so I had something to do. It was those kinds of grand gestures that endeared him not only to me but to other people too."

Mildred "Billie" Ligon Fatheree and Hal "Boss" Peterson were married at Boss's home on Morningside.

"I remember Mother handwriting the invitations," said Betty. "It was a small wedding with close friends and relatives. Guy Griggs was there . . . and Charlie Johnston. It was that kind of event. Mother was very happy, and so was Boss. I don't think Boss expected it to grow into the love that it was. I think it took him by surprise."

Later in his life, Boss surprised Betty Lee with his love for her children. "He was good with the grandkids. It was amazing how he tolerated their crying." As a distraction, he would say to the children, "Bingo, Bingo." And, as hard as it was for him physically, "Boss would sit on the floor and play with the grandchildren." Witnessing this relationship with her children, Betty wondered, "Would life have been different for Boss if he had his own children?"

From his youth, Charlie Peterson had the countenance, humor, and boyish looks that women adored. Charlie was first married to Lila Alice Haden on July 16, 1927. Lila came from "the coast" and was a patient at the Thompson TB Sanitarium. It is said that her family had money and that she was spoiled because she had been ill much of her life. Charlie and Lila moved to 705 W.

Main, the Westland Additions "dream house," as model homes were called in the 1920s. The "dream" was short-lived for Charlie and Lila.

Secretary Willa Mae said: "I always thought Charlie Peterson was one of the sweetest men I've ever been around, and I can't imagine anyone ever being unhappy with him, but she evidently was."

The marriage failed to connect, and Charlie returned to the life of a bachelor. Although there were always women wanting into his life, there remained a bachelor side of Charlie that caused him not to marry again until midlife.

Mabel Violet Peterson, born on May 9, 1921, was twenty years younger than Charlie. After divorcing her first husband, she had moved to Kerrville from Uvalde with her mother, Minnie Mae Barton. Violet had a daughter, Beverly Beuershausen, who was four years old when Violet met Charlie. Although she was never adopted by Charlie, Beverly always viewed Charlie as "the only father I ever had," and the two were very close.

Beverly (Beuershausen) Sullivan remembered Charlie walking up and down Water Street and visiting all of his relatives who owned the various businesses. One of them was cousin Carl Peterson, who owned American Pure Milk, located at that time along the west end of downtown.

When Charlie walked into "The Creamery" and saw Violet working there, said Sullivan, "it was love at first sight for both of them. . . . I am sure there were a lot of raised eyebrows in town when they married because here was Charlie Peterson, and he was definitely an older man, and she was a 'grass widow' (divorced) with a child in tow."

Charlie had to woo both the mother and daughter. "Just about one of my earliest memories in life is when Charlie showed up at our doorstep and pulled from his suitcoat pocket a tiny little Chihuahua. That got us off on a really good start," Sullivan recalled.

Charlie was in his early forties, Violet in her early twenties. They had both been married before, but something about her caused Charlie to drop his bachelor ways and settle down. Charlie's second marriage, to Violet, was the marriage to the love of his life. The couple wed in San Antonio at Y.O. Ranch owner Myrtle Schreiner's hotel apartment.

At this point in his life, Charlie was more than anxious to be a family man. The couple's first house was at 506 Elm Street in the Westland Addition, which Charlie and Boss had developed. While they lived on Elm Street, Violet became pregnant, but miscarried. Beverly Sullivan recalled it as a "very devastating time."

Charlie and Violet built a Tommy Noonan-designed house at 1217 Virginia Drive in Starkey Addition. This home was one of the first ranch-style homes in Kerrville. The house was so large that people stopped by during construction, mistaking it for Starkey Elementary School, which was also being built.

Tommy Noonan remembered one day when Boss came to the construction site of Charlie's new house. "Boss was asking how many square feet, who is doing this, and who is doing that. He made an observation that a fool and his money are soon parted. It was a good-natured thing, but he thought Charlie was spending more money than he ought to on the house."

Charlie and Violet, who often enjoyed driving to Mexico, lived at the home they built until Charlie died.

Sullivan describes Charlie as "the gentlest, most loving person . . . a real soft touch. Every time I would get sick, Charlie was my caretaker and my nurturer. He would go down to the drug store and buy me the latest Madame Alexander doll. The only time that man ever raised his voice to me was once when we were in Colorado riding horses, and I trotted my horse onto the pavement. Charlie just went crazy because it was a danger to the horse to run on pavement. It was the only time that man ever got mad at me.

"Uncle Boss could party hard. All three of those boys did. But Charlie had a sort of epiphany after he met my mother. He gave up the hard-living party ways," Sullivan said. "If you had to say which one was the most loved, it would be Charlie. If you had to say which one was the most admired for his business acumen, it would be Uncle Boss. Their personalities were totally different. Charlie was perfectly content to take a back seat to Uncle Boss.

"Charlie loved to play poker. His poker group consisted of everyone from the Schreiner brothers to guys who made deliveries. He had friends from all walks. There would have been no place for Charlie in a world of social snobs."

The third son of Sid "Cap" Peterson had returned to the family's ranch on the Divide west of Kerrville and refused to be confined by the business world. Joe Sid Peterson married Nora Blanchette in the late 1920s. The couple had one daughter, Nora Joe Peterson, born on September 14, 1930. After Nora and Joe Sid's divorce, responsibility for raising Nora Joe was left to Joe Sid. On April 13, 1947, he married a nurse from San Antonio, Mary Alice Donahoo, with whom he lived until his death.

"In the end," said one who knew the family well, "Boss and Joe Sid married women who would take care of them . . . and put up with them."

Kerrville old-timers said Joe Sid carried one of the friendliest attitudes and was "the nicest guy in the world." He was often described as "happy-go-lucky," unless he was drinking too much. Many admitted that "Joe Sid was an obnoxious drunk."

He enjoyed playing pranks, even on his very proper mother. Once he slipped a little nude statue on her hospital bedside table just before a visit by the preacher.

Like his two brothers, Joe Sid had the Peterson weakness of the heart. At his death on January 11, 1958, at age fifty-five, Joe Sid received the following tribute in the local newspaper:

> A native of Kerrville, he had grown to manhood in the city and on the Peterson ranches on the Divide. He attended school here and also the San Antonio Academy. He was a vigorous outdoor type of man and loved ranch life, and spent most of his time on the ranch or at his farm home, "Casa Pobre" (Poor House), along Turtle Creek on the Medina Road. That he was a man's man was evidenced by the large number of men who came from far and near to pay their respects to him as his body lay in state or to attend funeral services. He was loyal and most generous to his friends, who loved him dearly. . . . When his health would permit, he was an ardent sportsman and enjoyed hunting and fishing.

No one can be certain why brothers Boss and Charlie always joined in business partnerships, and yet brother Joe Sid never participated in the family businesses, except for the ranching interests. From all appearances, the three brothers remained equally close friends.

"Close?" said Boss's widow Billie. "You wouldn't know it, and the public wouldn't know it, but the brothers were close. Boss loved his family, and that's it."

But Joe Sid heard a call to be as wild and free as the game he loved to hunt. Hunting and fishing were passions Joe Sid shared with his other brothers, especially Charlie. Boss viewed hunting not as a sport but as a way to do more business. His business sense helped him to see the importance of conserving wild game and native lands.

As the century progressed, Texas Hill Country hunting became much more than a sport to the ranchers of the area, who were beginning to convert it into big business. For Boss Peterson, hunting and business became inexorably intertwined.

Early in his business life, Boss learned how to use the social side of life to enhance his business connections. At any party, Boss ruled the social atmosphere. A natural promoter, Boss was perhaps the ultimate party guest or host.

"If Boss went to a party," said attorney Joe Burkett, "Boss would know everybody at the party when it was over."

But he was not as gregarious away from a social gathering as one might suppose.

"He was not a very outgoing man to have done the things he did," Billie recalled.

The chain-smoking Boss was not himself a sportsman, and he didn't like to play cards. He did love to sit at a table and talk to whomever was handy. Many people who remember Boss have a visual image of him sitting behind a round table talking and listening to all kinds of people on any and every subject.

"He used the phone a lot," stepdaughter Betty Lee said. "He called my mother 'Baby' and I remember him saying, 'Baby, get me this number, get me that number.' He kept up with a network of friends through the telephone."

Boss also figured out that it was better for business to be the one throwing the party than it was to be only one who attended, and he became one of the biggest and most frequent entertaining hosts Texas had seen. His "parties" took place even when he was hospitalized or living in San Antonio hotels. It is said that the hotel management would occasionally request that Boss move to another hotel so the staff could recover.

To keep control as the host and to maximize his business contacts, Boss bought in 1940 a piece of land called Camp Eagle, from which he developed an entire ranch devoted to the business of business entertaining.

CHAPTER 7

Buying Small, Making Big

BOSS PETERSON HAD HIS first heart attack in the mid-1930s, when he was thirty-six years old.

In a family plagued with heart problems and uncertain life spans, Boss Peterson inherited the worst of the Peterson genes, and he compounded the genetics with a lifestyle of high pressure business battles, little exercise, weight problems, booze, and cigarettes (reportedly up to five packs a day at times).

Boss suffered from not only heart ailments but also diabetes, arthritis in his spine, which confined him to a wheelchair during the middle period of his life, and emphysema. Even his teeth gave him constant problems. He searched throughout his life for a dentist who could fit his false teeth properly.

From his thirties onward to his death, he lived a third of each year in hospitals, usually in San Antonio, and he conducted much of his business from a hospital bed. Pajamas and robe with house shoes became his business attire for months at a time. Periodically, he had to have his lungs pumped out since the fluid put even more pressure on an already weakened heart, and at least once he is said to have "flat line" died on the operating table of a San Antonio hospital.

Despite his health, visitors to his hospital room almost always found Boss joking, upbeat, playful.

Periodically, Boss would begin to feel that he would not live much longer. He was not a religious man, so he put his limited energy into making the most of whatever days he had.

Boss was "business twenty-four hours a day," as one associate put it, and he liked to have lots of people around him, mostly business associates. His favorite hobby was "listening to deals." He was described as a "certain type of Texas man who liked to play the good old boy and hoped to have a lot of money." Boss could be blunt, and he sometimes seemed a demigod who hid behind his wealth to those who knew him only casually.

He was indeed a legend in his own lifetime. Few people of any consequence in South Texas had not heard of the powerful and mysterious Boss Peterson.

Perhaps because of his health problems, perhaps because of his "big picture" nature, perhaps because he inherited his father's knack of sizing up people, Boss early on had developed a particular style of business.

"I like to buy small," he said. "I make big."

Recalled George Delavan, a partner in Boss's developments in San Antonio, "It was the finest thing to be a member of Boss's team. He would employ you, then leave you alone. He worked for fun. When we had business meetings, I would often die laughing with him."

Delavan remembered a meeting where a businessman who was seeking an investment from Boss said there were six reasons why Boss should get into the deal. The first one, the businessman explained, was cash, and he outlined the cash flow.

Before the businessman could list the other five reasons, Boss said: "That's reason enough. We'll do it."

An optimist, Boss had an impulsive nature which is not always best in business dealings, so he tempered his tendency with a partnership which placed controls upon his enthusiasm.

Boss used his brother, Charlie, as a restraint to keep him from bolting too soon, associates said. Charlie rarely spent much time in the office. In fact, Charlie didn't even get assigned an office at Peterson Interests during one remodeling. When asked where Charlie was located, one employee reportedly responded, "He's in our hearts."

Attorney Joe Burkett described Charlie as "quiet, easy going, smart, and tough as a bolt. You didn't run over Charlie Peterson."

Secretary Willa Mae spoke of Charlie's role: "Charlie never dictated a letter in his life. Not a business letter. I did do a few things for him, but they were personal. Charlie didn't get excited about the ranches, the automobile business, the tire testing. He just lived his quiet life and went about his own business. He was agreeable to anything Hal wanted to do."

Charlie walked the streets of downtown Kerrville and kept Peterson Interests in touch with the town's small businesses and common man.

The two of them used first lieutenant Guy Griggs for even more common-sense restraint. Most business deals were said to have been constructed with Boss owning 49 percent of the deal and Charlie owning 49 percent. Griggs was given 2 percent. If the two brothers agreed, the 2 percent vote of Griggs meant nothing. But if the overly optimistic Boss proposed a deal about which Charlie had reservations, Griggs's 2 percent could keep Boss in check. There are indications that Griggs's 2 percent kept Boss from making a number of business deals which most likely would have gone sour.

This arrangement appears to have been incredibly successful because most of the business ventures made this way turned out winners for Peterson Interests. Boss got the deals going with the understanding that Griggs would keep the deals going—profitably.

Some deals that Boss made outside this arrangement were much less lucrative, even failures.

Those who worked with the three men remember the Kerrville Yellow Taxi Cab Company as an example. Boss's companies made the buses, rode the bus routes, sold and repaired automobiles, tested cars, hauled fuel and livestock. It made sense to Boss that he also should own the three local taxi cab companies. After all, his model was the vertical monopoly of Standard Oil. But Charlie had his doubts and was cool on the idea. Guy Griggs had the swing vote. After looking at the financial statements, Griggs pronounced the proposed taxi company a perpetual loser.

Usually, Boss listened to Charlie's and Guy's opinions, but on this occasion, Boss insisted on buying the taxi companies anyway.

Attorney Burkett remembered a day when Boss telephoned him and said, "Joe, can you come down here? I want to talk to you."

Burkett found Boss sitting at his desk with his hat on. "Boss had been drinking a little, and he said, 'I just bought the taxi companies. Louis "Tiny" Klein is going to manage them. I want you to incorporate this outfit.' Then Boss signed about five or six checks, and he instructed me to close the deals."

On his way out, Burkett walked by secretary Willa Mae's desk and asked to see Griggs. "I asked Guy, what about this taxi business?" Burkett said. "Guy said, 'Get the hell out of here. I don't want anything to do with that taxi business. That's up to you and Boss.' Guy never set foot in one of Boss's taxi cabs."

Even worse, Guy was right. In more than a decade of ownership by Boss, the taxi cabs never turned a profit. From all accounts, Charlie and Guy never let Boss hear the end of the taxi business. But Peterson's Auto Company did sell the taxi company new vehicles.

"Griggs didn't always agree with Boss, and they had some pretty good conversations," Burkett said. "Charlie was the balance wheel. Boss was the go-go operator. Boss had more ideas than a dog has fleas, and most of them were good."

When Willa Mae was asked about the taxi business, she laughed: "I never will forget that deal. It was a pain. Mr. Griggs never had anything to do with Yellow Cab Company. That was Boss's baby."

Despite his health problems, Boss kept pushing to grow his companies. One can only imagine what Boss might have accomplished if he had had the health of a normal man.

Even though the business must have been slowed by Boss's hospital stays, the companies comprising the Peterson Interests were creating great wealth by the end of the 1930s.

CHAPTER 8

The Golden Touch

THE GREAT DEPRESSION HAD sucked the capital out of America and most of the world, and the better part of a decade was required to restore the fuel of industry.

The depression that socked the nation's factory workers was perhaps a little easier to endure in the rural communities, which had more agrarian economies. After all, the farming or ranching family normally survived with very little cash passing through its pockets. The farm family owed the bank and the general store, so the autumn harvest involved a transfer of dollars which the farmer or rancher might hold in his own hand for less than a day. Unlike a city cousin who lost everything when the factory closed, the farm family still had food to eat and shelter from the elements.

The rural communities also seemed to face the Great Depression with a sense of togetherness, and this proved particularly true in the Texas Hill Country. The banks strained to keep the business and ranching communities intact. The employees sacrificed to keep their companies afloat.

Stories abound of the kindness of the Peterson Interests in those hard times, and the Petersons also benefited from the loyalty of their workers, their banks, and their supporters.

"Boss had a lot of friends who were bankers," recalled a San Antonio business partner. "He insisted that we put some of our deposits with bankers in the different little towns around the Hill Country. He wanted to scratch the backs of his friends and help them if he could."

Somehow Boss Peterson managed to keep his companies alive during the 1930s, and indeed, he even expanded many of them. Late in the decade, he found himself perfectly poised for the ending of the economic slump. As the nation's economy recovered, the Peterson Interests began to churn out the immense profits Boss had visualized.

In particular, Kerrville Bus Company had expanded its reach when the depression had proved too much for other competitors. Being able to grow during the worst economic decade in American history provided the springboard for Kerrville Bus Company to soar skyward as the economy turned and times improved.

When World War II broke out in Europe and engulfed the world, bus companies found themselves suddenly swamped with business. This was especially true in Texas, with its large number of military bases, its vast distances, and the wartime rationing of gasoline and automobile tires.

In the book *Intercity Bus Lines of the Southwest,* author Jack Rhodes describes the era in this manner:

> World War II had a profound effect on the Texas intercity bus industry. Most of the bus manufacturers saw their plants converted to wartime production for military needs. Parts were scarce, and qualified mechanics were in demand by the armed forces. The War Production Board and the Office of Defense Transportation curtailed many expendable routes and requisitioned the buses. Despite these restrictions, however, the bus lines of the state and the nation handled a vastly increased load of passengers.
>
> Both drivers and passengers who recall this era remember the hectic commotion of depots, the frequent breakdowns on the highway, and the general agony involved in getting anywhere. Soldiers were willing to ride in luggage racks and baggage bins to get to a larger town on a weekend pass. Mothers, wives, and girlfriends of servicemen traveled patiently across the state to spend even a few moments with the soldiers. Passenger loads were frequently "standing room only," and the extraordinary delays in allegedly "scheduled" departures were routine. One veteran driver told of pulling into the San Antonio depot in 1943, only to

have the press of humanity rip the entrance door off the bus, causing a two-hour delay of his already tardy departure for Dallas.

The war brought an increase in bus patrons soaring nationwide from 8.7 billion passenger miles in 1939 to 32.9 billion passenger miles by 1944.

The depression deal Boss made to form the Beck Company of Ohio proved brilliant. Perhaps because of its smaller size, the Beck Company was one of the few manufacturers which was not pressed into wartime production and continued to produce a significant volume of buses, many of which came into the Texas market since the Petersons owned one-third of the company. But because resources and bus production were limited by the war, many bus companies scrambled to purchase even the reduced number of coaches which Beck was able to manufacture.

In *RFD: The Changing Face of Rural America*, author Wayne E. Fuller wrote about the Beck buses:

> These buses left much to be desired on the road and in the shop. The riding quality was among the worst. Road calls were frequent, and the buses were under-powered. The mechanics did not like to work on them due to the non-standardized components, such as brakes. In all fairness to Beck, most of the deficiencies in these vehicles can probably be traced to the lack of parts and components available to Beck for manufacturing into a bus. Beck buses otherwise held a highly satisfactory judgment in the eyes of many, many bus lines over the years.

As Beck-made buses departed often with double the number of passengers for which they were designed, the Kerrville Bus Company prospered.

And so did the Peterson's Garage and Auto Company, which later came to be known as Hill Country Motors before being sold to San Antonio auto dealer Tom Benson in the 1970s.

Charlie Johnston, the nephew of Boss's first wife Dora, managed the auto company for decades. His contact was mainly with Guy Griggs, who "looked after" the Kerrville businesses for Boss.

"It was an all-ethical, goodwill operation," Johnston said. "I made my living for many years selling cars to the same people over and over."

Johnston once thought about buying another business, but he was cautioned by Charlie Peterson not to do so. "I don't think you ought to do that," Charlie told Johnston. "Some day you'll be running this whole outfit (the auto company)."

By entertaining and courting executives of General Motors, Boss had succeeded in doing what few other auto dealers were able to accomplish: He landed the franchise for all GM products and Jeeps. Even in the sparsely populated Hill Country, this allowed the Peterson dealership to be one of the most successful in the state.

In the months before World War II, Boss parlayed another aspect of the transportation business into a new idea for a company. The West Texas Auto Company organized on January 2, 1941, as the nation began to prepare to be enveloped by the war in Europe and Asia. The company used the winding, empty roads of the Hill Country and southwest Texas for the proving of tires along eight separate and distinctly different testing routes.

Ben Hyde, Sr., one of the drivers, said he was laid off after an accident. "They had a rule when you were driving for the test fleet. If you had a wreck, you were automatically laid off. I ran into Boss in Fredericksburg, and Boss asked, 'What are you doing here?' I replied that I got laid off this morning. Boss said, 'You go back over there and tell that fool to let you go back to work.' I said, 'No, you go back and tell them.' " By the time Hyde returned to Kerrville, he had his job back.

During the war years, the company put U.S. Army half-tracks through proving programs, and other tests were done for the U.S. Signal Corps. The company used the technical resources and manpower of Peterson's Auto Company to support a fleet of test vehicles. In its embryonic stage in 1941, the company tested with three automobiles and two trucks. Some twenty-five years later, this test fleet had grown to forty vehicles from passenger cars to heavy tandem trucks and employed 125 drivers. The tests roared down West Texas roads at 80 MPH in some areas—the Texas speed limit at the time was 60 MPH—with drivers working eight-hour shifts, twenty-four hours a day, six days a week. Even today, old-time Hill Country residents can remember the sound of the half-tracks rumbling down the roads.

The Texas Hill Country was ideal for proving tires because, as a tire manufacturer magazine article noted in 1958: "To check tread wear, tires are mounted on a fleet of test cars and trucks and are run on highways and roads of all types, mostly in and around Kerrville, Texas. This south Texas location was chosen for road tests because test drivers can operate at legal high speeds for hours with a minimum of traffic interference. The roads around Kerrville are open year round."

In the Peterson management style, West Texas Auto Company included many of the same faces that Boss relied on to "look after" other businesses: Guy G. Griggs, who "looked after" the Peterson Interests in Kerrville, became president; Charles H. Johnston, who "looked after" the auto dealership, was vice president and general manager; J. D. Mahaffey, who "looked after" the Kerrville Bus Company, was secretary-treasurer; Dick Staudt, who "looked after" West Texas Auto from its conception, was fleet supervisor; and a young John Milford Mosty, who later became secretary-treasurer-manager of the Hal and Charlie Peterson Foundation, became office manager.

The company tested for the biggest names in tires, including the B. F. Goodrich Company, Kelly-Springfield Tire Company, Dunlop Tire and Rubber, Dayton Tire and Rubber, Gates Rubber Company, Atlas Supply Company, Chace Rubber Company, Mohawk Rubber Company, Oldberg Manufacturing, Western Auto, and McCreary Tire and Rubber.

During the war years, Boss also formed Texas Transport, a company which transported petroleum, and he bought and sold a number of other companies, many transportation-related, which increased the wealth of the Peterson Interests. Boss purchased Schreiner Wool and Mohair and KERV Radio in Kerrville from the Hill Country's famed Schreiner family. The Peterson Interests also got into the subdivision boom after the war by developing the Hillcrest Addition and Westland Development Company Subdivision in Kerrville.

Dick Staudt, who managed the tire testing company, wanted to build a house in the Westland Addition, but first he had to sell his house on Hugo Street. Dick had been trying to negotiate a sale with a neighbor who owned all the land around the Hugo Street house. When Dick told Boss that the negotiations were not going very well, Boss responded that he would be meeting with the man that evening. "We are going to do some trading tonight, so you come over for one drink and then say you have to go to work," Boss told Dick. The following morning Dick learned that Boss had included Dick's house in the negotiations. Boss not only sold Dick's house to the neighbor, but he got $3,800 more than Dick had been asking originally.

Boss knew how to weave business deals together and use his power to get what he wanted.

"Boss coveted monopoly," said Kerrville attorney Joe Burkett. "Boss used to say that the fellow who invented monopoly was a first cousin to the guy who invented interest."

During World War II (and indeed even today), a high percentage of America's military personnel passed through San Antonio for training. Boss, who was spending several months of the year in San Antonio, decided that all those soldiers in their new starched uniforms with close haircuts and nice smiles presented a business opportunity. Every one of them required a soldier portrait to send home to family and friends. He capitalized on the timing, using his photographic company, Beverly Studios in San Antonio. "Besides having all the military base contracts, we also had every school contract in the area as well as the annual contract to take pictures of the students at Hockaday Girls School in Dallas," said Frank Stanush, who oversaw Beverly Studios for Boss.

In 1942, Frank Stanush was a twenty-six-year-old aspiring artist who worked in the advertising department for Interstate Theaters in San Antonio. Jobs were very hard to find in those days, and Stanush was thankful to have a "meager income" from the movie job.

Frank saw Boss's golden palomino horse named Pleasant King in its silver saddle at the rodeo in San Antonio, and Stanush wanted to breed a horse he owned. Architect Tommy Thompson, a mutual acquaintance, took Stanush to the Menger Hotel to meet Boss so Stanush could inquire about "buying" the stud fee for Pleasant King.

Boss laughed and said, "What makes you think it is for sale?"

Stanush turned on his heels to leave the room, but before he reached the door, Boss said, "Young man, what do you do for a living?" When Stanush responded that he was an artist for the movie theaters, Boss asked Stanush to paint a picture of Pleasant King.

Then, in true Boss fashion, he presented Stanush with a deal: If Boss liked the picture, Boss would trade it for the stud fee. Stanush went to Diamond Bar Ranch and painted the picture. Boss got his portrait of Pleasant King, and Stanush got a horse.

"Boss was able to visualize how I could work into his operation by doing art work and promotion for his horses and his dogs," Stanush said. A few months later, Boss asked Stanush to work at the photography studio.

It proved a tough decision for the young man. "I was very conservative and scared to leave my job," Stanush said, but he never regretted going into business with Boss Peterson.

The man who was running the studio was embezzling from Boss, and Boss knew it. When Stanush took over the studio, the business was $6,000 in debt, in addition to the $6,000 Boss had paid for the business.

"It was not a big business," Stanush said. "At that time, it was a small shop at 1411 North Main. Boss asked me where the finest photographers in the U.S. were at work, and I told him that they were in Hollywood, Chicago, New York, and Philadelphia. Boss said that he would set up some money for me to buy a plane ticket to all of those cities. He wanted me to study the best and put their techniques into practice here."

Stanush was most impressed with the glamour photography being done in Hollywood at the movie studios. "I was able to make sketches of the examples of photography and brought an armload of those back to San Antonio," he said. When he returned to Texas, Stanush coined the name "Beverly Studios" to imply Hollywood glamour.

Soon Beverly Studios had created the cadet photo center at Lackland military base. Boss had a close friend named Judge Henry Burney who introduced Stanush to the colonel at the post exchange to show the Hollywood-style photography display samples. The colonel was impressed, which gave the business a foothold at the base. Big samples of the Hollywood knock-off photos displayed in the Main Street studio window also began drawing the local business.

"We went in for glamour photography, and that's what made us such a hit. We were soon doing more photographic business than anybody in San Antonio. Even Boss was amazed we became so successful," Stanush said. "My brother Claude was in Hollywood as a *Life Magazine* correspondent at the time I went out there to do research. Claude opened the doors at the movie studios for me."

Boss expected Beverly Studios to serve as a tax write-off. The young, eager-to-please Stanush wanted to make the studio a success. "At the end of the first year, I proudly showed Boss the financial statement. We had made $27,000 clear and had paid off the original $12,000 debt. Boss looked at me over his thick glasses and said, 'You really played hell. I'm in a 92 percent tax bracket, and I have to stick money someplace else because over 90 of what you (Beverly Studios) make goes to the government, and you don't have enough capital to continue.' So we quickly made the business a corporation.

"We really kept going with that business," Stanush continued. "We eventually had thirteen studios at different locations in Oklahoma, Louisiana, and Texas. We had 150 employees, and we reached the point where we were doing a million and a half in volume."

Beverly Studios lasted a long time (from 1942 to 1972). Boss made Stanush a 20 percent partner, then a 50 percent partner. "Boss was a big interest to me," Stanush said, "but the photography business never did become that important to me. When Boss became very ill, he called me and asked if I wanted to buy the other 50 percent. I said it wouldn't be any interest to me, but I did buy it from the estate after he died.

"Boss was a man before his time," Stanush recalled. "Boss could have remained wrapped up in the Texas Hill Country, but he had an interest in the outside world long before business had gone global. Having a lot of money helped Boss fill this image and allowed him to sort of wink at life. He laughed off his heart attacks and filled his life with lots of people around him.

"I loved Boss. He deeply changed my life," said Stanush. "It was a delight to work with Boss. There was no college education that would have compared with the association that I had with him."

Stanush managed the photography business nineteen years for Boss, and he got to know Boss very well in the last years of his life. Stanush went on to business success after Boss died, using the vertical integration concept which he learned from his association with Boss.

In the late 1930s and 1940s, the Peterson Interests turned almost every business opportunity into a success. Boss indeed had the golden touch. In the midst of these business triumphs, Boss tossed in $100 and formed a charitable foundation with brother Charlie.

Above left: *The Charlie Peterson family. Charlie with wife Violet and stepdaughter Beverly, and beloved dog "Woofus," a gift from Charlie to Beverly.*

Above right: *Violet and Beverly Peterson before Violet's marriage to Charlie and at a time when he was "wooing his soon-to-be stepdaughter."*

Lower right: *Violet Peterson on right with friend.*

Top left: *Audrey Ralls, Hal Peterson's second wife.*

Top right: *Left to right: Colonel Peacock with his wife, Hal Peterson, and Dorothy Stanush.*

Below left: *Ranch hand brings in an extra saddle horse at Camp Eagle.*

Below right: *W. C. Fawcett, Charlie Peterson, and Dick Flach playing cards.*

Left: *One of the fine palominos sold by Hal Peterson.*

Right: *Hal Peterson captured in a rare moment on top of Pleasant King in 1941. The picture was signed, "To my best friend Guy Griggs with best wishes, Hal Peterson."*

Bottom: *Ben Hyde, Sr., ready to deliver palomino horses for the Peterson Interests.*

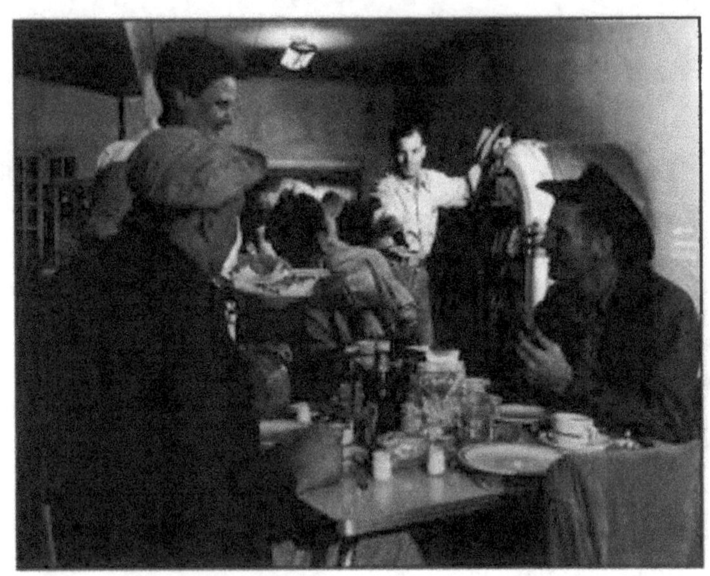

Top: *West Texas Auto Company tire test drivers taking a late night break at Five Points Café in Kerrville, Texas.*

Middle: *West Texas Auto Company tire fleet testing car hits the Hill Country roads.*

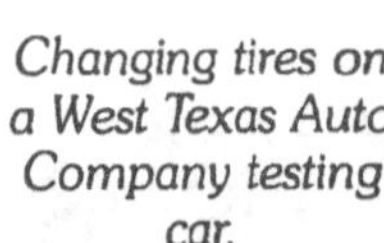
Changing tires on a West Texas Auto Company testing car.

Top: *Group photo of West Texas Auto tire test drivers in 1948. Dick Staudt is standing in the front row on the right.*

A West Texas Auto Company car crosses the "old" Kerrville bridge headed toward the Sid Peterson Memorial Hospital in the background and downtown. The hospital was under construction at the time.

A technician of West Texas Auto Company with an army half track disassembled.

The Kerrville Bus Company is on the move with a new Beck Twin Level model.

Boss Peterson standing with cane in front of a Kerrville Bus. Left to right, Rufus Mathews, J. D. Mahaffey, Mr. Wilshire, Boss, and unknown man.

Secretaries and office workers at the Kerrville Bus Company. Front row on right is Willa Mae Gibson, longtime personal secretary of Boss and Guy Griggs.

Above: *An early Kerrville Bus Company bus on an Austin to Houston run.*

Below: *1939 Kerrville Bus Company bus.*

Above: *1929 Kerrville Bus Fleet.*

Middle: *Memories of WWII. Army half tracks were a familiar sight and sound in the Texas Hill Country during the 1940s.*

Bottom: *Hal Peterson shaking hands with Frank Watts, the general sales manager of Humble Oil. Left to right: Charles Demsey, unknown, Frank Watts, Guy Griggs, unknown, Hal Peterson, and Charles Johnston.*

Joe Sid and Mary Peterson (second and third from the left) with hunters.

Left: *Joe Sid Peterson with daughter Nora Joe and wife Mary shopping in San Antonio.*

A Beverly Photography Studios delivery car.

Brother Joe Sid Peterson in front of the Diamond Bar Ranch home.

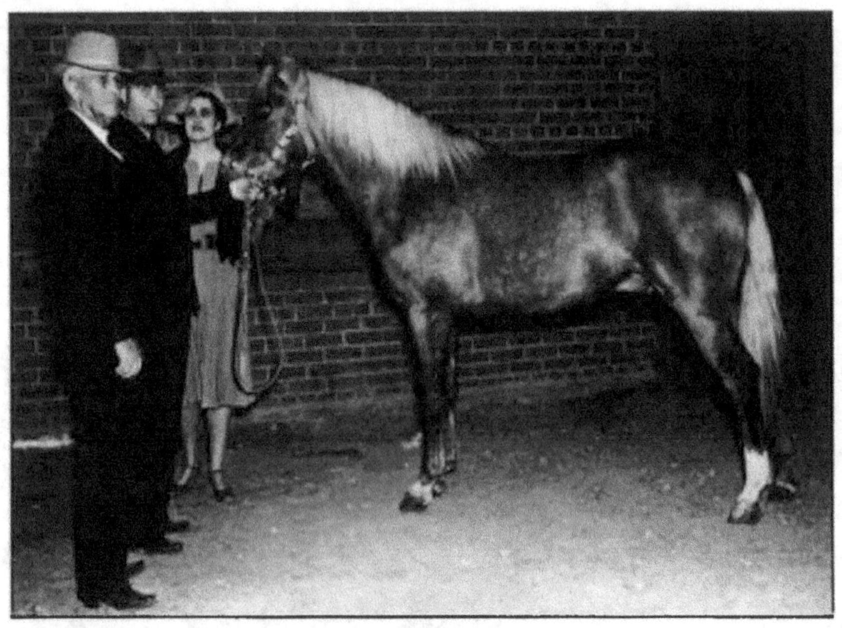

Above: *Sid "Cap" Peterson with Hal and wife Dora Johnston Peterson standing with one of their "golden" palominos.*

Mr. and Mrs. Hal (and Audrey) Peterson's home in Westland Addition, in Kerrville, Texas.

Left: *Hal Peterson's beloved wife Dora with his stepdaughter Kathleen.*

Hal Peterson's first wife, Dora Johnston.

Photo taken at the Menger Hotel in San Antonio during one of Hal Peterson's parties. Left to right, Congressman Tom Kilday, President of Pearl Brewery Datus Proper, and Frank Stanush.

Both photos examples of the Beverly Studios glamour photo technique.

PART THREE

The Gift

Above: *Artist watercolor of Sid Peterson Memorial Hospital painted in 1949 by E. M. Schiwetz.*

Below: *July 1949, the Sid Peterson Memorial Hospital prepares for the grand opening ceremonies.*

CHAPTER 9

A New Hospital

THE COMMUNITY OF KERRVILLE has always benefited from the love it has elicited from its residents.

From its outset, the town has received great charity from its business and civic leaders, and has rarely paid for lands for schools or recreational facilities which have proved burdens for taxpayers of other cities.

The first mayor, Capt. Joseph A. Tivy, donated almost seventeen acres of land for the first school in 1890, and he gave the school district enough additional land to pay for the first building. But building lots were not selling all that fast in Kerrville in the late 1890s, so the schools issued thirty-eight-year bonds to finance the building until the lots could be sold. The name of Tivy High School still honors the generosity of Captain Tivy.

Capt. Charles Schreiner donated the land for Schreiner College, a private school affiliated with the Presbyterian Church, and L. A. Schreiner gave the lands for the school's football field and little league field. Mrs. A. L. Starkey, Sr., contributed land for the construction of Starkey Elementary School.

The Butt family, which started the H-E-B Grocery Company with one small store in Kerrville, established the striking Butt-Holdsworth Memorial Library overlooking the Guadalupe River.

Boss Peterson was known to have been taken with the donation by Robert P. Hayes of thirty-five acres of river bottom land to the City of Kerrville, and he actively participated in the one-day blitz of workers which turned this bend in the river into the downtown Louise Hays Park. Named for Robert's wife, the park is as fine an asset as any city could ever hope to possess.

Secretary Willa Mae remembered: "Boss got the idea about building the park. As usual, he wanted it done now. The city and Mr. Peterson called in every bulldozer in the country and everybody they could find, and they built that park in one day." Two thousand volunteers turned out, and the "park that was built in a day" made the cover of *Life Magazine*.

Few communities ever see such charitable support.

But the jewel in Kerrville's crown of generosity is the Sid Peterson Memorial Hospital, a gift to the Texas Hill Country from Hal and Charlie Peterson.

With the Peterson heart problem hanging over the family, Boss had plenty of opportunity to think about hospitals. After his first heart attack in 1936, he never escaped the sterile-smelling, cheerfully painted hospital hallways for very long at a time. Most years he spent one-fourth to one-third of his time confined in one.

Sid "Cap" Peterson died from heart disease in a San Antonio hospital in the fall of 1939, and it was about that time when Dr. Leon Kopecky remembered first discussing the idea of a Kerrville hospital with Boss.

Dr. Kopecky had known Boss since he arrived in San Antonio for a hospital stay in 1936, and someone told the doctor that he should get to know "that very interesting man from Kerrville." The doctor did take time to meet and befriend Boss, and he would serve as his physician for the remainder of Peterson's life. "Boss did a lot of things people didn't know about," said Dr. Kopecky. "He used to send me patients, and at the end of the month, the bills would be paid by him.

"Boss was a man born into middle age," the doctor added. "He was never nineteen or twenty years old. He had the most terrific retention. You only had to tell him something one time."

When Boss was in the hospital, the entire mood of the floor changed into a combination of business and party atmosphere with streams of people coming and going from the southwest corner private room he insisted on turning into an office and living room. As long as he paid, Boss could and did stay in the hospital as long as he wanted.

"I had Boss in the hospital up to three months at a time," Dr. Kopecky said. "I finally figured out why he would stay at the hospital. One of the reasons is that he wouldn't drink. Another is that everyone knew where he was. He had a telephone and a nurse, and he did more business out of the hospital than he ever did anywhere else because he could give it nearly 100 percent of his time. You never knew who would be in his room. Boss would sit in his robe and listen to deals all day long, taking them apart piece by piece. He had a very fertile mind and was always thinking ten miles ahead of everyone else."

Boss would be in his wheelchair or in his bed as he talked, the doctor said, in a very relaxed manner which effectively hid the hard-charger who resided beneath the surface. Boss would insist on giving the doctor money to sneak out and buy him some ham and eggs, prohibited by his diet.

One evening, Dr. Kopecky listened for a couple of hours as Boss rubbed his forehead and complained about Kerrville's "old rattletrap hospital." Perhaps Boss was feeling particularly mortal that night, and Dr. Kopecky began to discuss the Kerrville hospital.

"I've got to do something for Kerrville," the doctor remembered that Boss suddenly exclaimed. "Let's build a hospital."

The only general hospital in Kerrville was the Secor Hospital, founded in 1911 by Dr. William Secor, who came to the Hill Country in search of a drier climate for his arthritis. Secor opened his practice in a small rock building on the corner of Sidney Baker and Main streets. He added to the building in 1914 and in the 1920s, and he built an extensive surgical practice in the small hospital which had grown inadequate for a town the size of Kerrville.

By the 1940s, Secor Hospital is said to have contained only an X-ray machine and very little else. The medical staff was elderly and not anxious to change, old-timers remember, and some of the doctors were not happy that a new and modern hospital might be built in Kerrville.

Boss asked Kopecky if he knew any architects who specialized in building hospitals, and Kopecky answered no, but the doctor had read an article in *Reader's Digest* about an architect who designed hospitals. Boss called the architect, who flew down for a meeting in which Boss recorded the architect's ideas on a tape recorder.

In Boss's mind, the hospital project was under way. Once he had an idea, Boss often showed impatience to get it done as he assigned the work to those around him. A man with a very serious heart condition who chain smokes cigarettes through a long cigarette holder must know he does not have a long time to accomplish his goals.

But the looming world war meant that nothing concrete could be accomplished for several years.

Carl Meek, a Kerrville real estate salesman who once worked for Peterson Auto, described Kerrville at the brink of World War II as a sleepy little town just starting to wake up. A few tourists were moving in up and down the river, but basically the town of 9,000 people lived off agriculture and hunting.

As the war years came, Kerrville Bus Company showed incredible profits, most of which were sucked out of the Texas Hill Country and pulled into Washington, D.C., by the excess profits tax. Boss hated that 92 percent tax bracket.

He gathered his inner circle together and began to discuss the idea of a charitable foundation which would build a hospital. An important consideration for Boss was that this plan would keep money earned in the Texas Hill Country *in* the Texas Hill Country. To some extent, Boss and Charlie could control what happened to the profits instead of seeing the money disappear into the black hole of federal taxes.

His idea was that the Petersons would build a hospital which would prevent Kerr County taxpayers from having to do so. It had become increasingly apparent that this would have to happen if the Hill Country was to have first-class medical facilities.

Boss thought he would be able to put many of his assets in this proposed foundation because, as a man who had barely survived three heart attacks, he had virtually no life expectancy. He could not buy life insurance. "I can prove to the IRS that I have no life expectancy," Boss said.

Periodically, Boss would begin to feel that he would not be able to live much longer, so he approached his projects with a sense of urgency.

By the early 1940s, both Boss and Charlie had reached

middle-age with diminishing prospects of leaving an heir. Privately, Hal and Charlie must have mutually agreed to leave the bulk of their wealth to the foundation that they were creating. As it was with all agreements between the two brothers, this decision was unwritten and perhaps even unstated. But it was as binding as their word, and despite changing circumstances later in life which might have caused other men to divert their estates elsewhere, the brothers endowed the foundation through their lives and through their deaths.

Because the nation's resources were almost completely devoted to the war effort in the early 1940s, little could be done to build a hospital until the end of the war came into sight. On Halloween of 1944, the following charter was signed:

> Know all men by these present: That we, Hal Peterson, Charlie Peterson, Guy G. Griggs, C. H. Gilmer and Henry P. Burney, all citizens of Texas, under and by virtue of the laws of the State of Texas do hereby voluntarily associate ourselves for the purpose of forming a private corporation under such laws upon the following terms and conditions:
>
> The name of the corporation shall be: "Hal and Charlie Peterson Foundation."
>
> The purpose for which this corporation is formed is the support of any charitable or educational undertaking as authorized by Subdivision 2 of Article 1302 of the Revised Civil Statutes of Texas of 1925. Such purposes shall always be limited to and exclusively for public or charitable or educational purposes in the State of Texas, and no part of the earnings or assets of this corporation shall ever inure to the benefit of any private shareholder or individual, and no part of the activities of this corporation shall be to carry on propaganda, or otherwise to attempt to influence legislation.
>
> This corporation shall have the power to take and receive gifts and bequests or real and/or personal property as are within its purposes, and may have and hold by purchase such property, and shall have all such other powers and privileges that such corporations have and are given under the laws of the State of Texas.
>
> The places the business of this corporation is to be transacted are in Kerrville, Kerr County, Texas, and elsewhere within the State of Texas in accordance with the laws of Texas, and its principal place of business is to be in said City of Kerrville, Texas.
>
> The term for which this corporation is to exist is fifty (50) years.

> The number of trustees shall be five (5), and the names and residences of those who are appointees for the first year are as follows:
>
> Hal Peterson, Kerrville, Texas,
> Charlie Peterson, Kerrville, Texas,
> Guy G. Griggs, Kerrville, Texas,
> C. H. Gilmer, Kerrville, Texas,
> Henry P Burney, San Antonio, Texas.
>
> In the case of any vacancy in the board of trustees through death, resignation, disqualification or other cause, the remaining trustees by affirmative vote of a majority may elect a successor to hold office for the unexpired portion of the term of the trustee whose place is vacant, and until the election of a successor.
>
> A majority of the trustees shall constitute a quorum and shall have power to elect and employ officers, provide for filling vacancies, to make all necessary by-laws for the government of this corporation and the regulation of its affairs and the management of its property, and to transact all of its business, and to do and perform all necessary acts to carry into effect the purposes of this corporation.
>
> This corporation shall not have any capital stock and does not at this time own any goods, chattels, lands, rights or credits, except the sum of $100 cash which has been donated to this corporation by Hal Peterson, one of the incorporators.

Beginning only with the $100 which Boss chunked into the kitty, this group of men set out to build a hospital which would cost three-quarters of a million dollars. The Hal and Charlie Peterson Foundation began without mention of any hospital, but it was always the major goal. And the Foundation began in Kerrville with little fanfare. Nothing in the newspaper marked its beginning. Few people shared the vision that Boss had for the hospital and even fewer, probably very few, ever thought that Boss's dream would actually come true. It was far too grandiose, too risky of an idea to contemplate that these two Kerrville ranchers could build and sustain a million-dollar charitable medical facility with little or no assistance from the public.

Typical of the Petersons' operating style, the Foundation board was a close-knit group with the power to self-perpetuate this continued closeness. Fifty years later, some might not understand why Hal and Charlie would keep membership of the Foundation board so closely held, but it was typical of those days for a handful of well-heeled leaders to serve as an oligarchy for their town. This style was common for prominent wealthy pioneer families, their businesses, and their foundations.

While Boss and Charlie wanted to build a hospital for the community, they also wanted to keep enough control on the almost $1 million they donated to be certain it would be appropriated as Boss desired. Both were non-public men who wanted to keep their financial dealings as private as possible. This explains why there were so few press accounts of the Petersons' business and charitable activities. Their passion to be private gave the Peterson Foundation almost an anonymous air of mystery that lasted for decades despite the high-profile hospital.

The first meeting of the Foundation's trustees came on July 23, 1945, when the Foundation unanimously elected Hal Peterson as chairman and Guy G. Griggs as secretary. Then the corporation was formed, by-laws were adopted, and officers elected. Hal Peterson was elected president; Charlie Peterson became vice president; and Guy G. Griggs became secretary-treasurer. The board voted to deposit moneys of the corporation in Chas. Schreiner Bank in Kerrville.

The corporation next began looking for a site on which to build a new hospital. Boss had a location in mind along the river just below downtown. About the same time, Houston lawyer Charlie Reinhardt purchased the property, Peterson employee Mrs. Garland Scogin remembered, and Reinhardt wanted more for his new property than Boss was willing to pay. The transaction never occurred, and the property still has not been developed decades later.

Other possible sites were on the edges of the city, an idea Boss never liked.

Hired as architects were Addis E. Noonan and his son, Tommy A. Noonan. Addis had built the Blue Yodeler House for Jimmie Rodgers in Kerrville, and he had designed a house for Boss and his first wife, Dora, located at 614 W. Main. Son Tommy later went on to design the ranch-style house for Charlie and his second wife, Violet.

The hospital's father and son architects strongly argued for a purer location at the edge of town where the grounds and landscaping could complement their design and make the solving of problems like hospital access and parking much easier. Tommy Noonan, who had just come back from the service, was to supervise the construction. Other architects employed included Jack Finney, who had been a senior professor of architecture at Texas A&M, and Thomas B. Thompson, who also had been a professor in A&M's junior architectural class. Finney, in particular, was assigned to work directly under the elder Noonan in developing the original design of the facility, according to Tommy Noonan. Finney kept urging the senior Noonan to persuade Boss not to build the hospital downtown, but Boss wanted the hospital patterned after the Nix Hospital in downtown San Antonio, where Boss had spent a great deal of his adult life. The Nix also had rental property on the ground level to provide income to help subsidize the maintenance of the hospital.

If one steps back to examine Sid Peterson Memorial Hospital jammed into crowded downtown Kerrville today, one might conclude that the architects were right: a location with space would have been better. But Boss had a unique viewpoint of what a hospital should be. Because he spent so much time in hospitals, perhaps Boss mostly viewed a hospital from the perspective of a regular occupant. He spent his life trying to be comfortable in hospitals, trying to do business out of hospitals, trying to remain an integral part of the community while confined to a hospital bed, room, and hallway. To Boss, the idea of a hospital out in the country meant that its patients would be cut off from the life of Kerrville. To Boss, a hospital should be right in the middle of the town, literally the heart of the community, and he was determined to keep the facility close to downtown.

With politicians arguing against his ideas and architects expressing their reservations, the path of least resistance would have been to place the hospital on the outskirts of Kerrville. But Boss never allowed opposition from smaller men to obstruct his goals. After making no headway fighting the politics of the day for a site near downtown, Boss said, "Hell, I'll build the hospital on land I already own."

So that is how the Hal and Charlie Peterson Foundation came to build a hospital in the absolute heart of downtown Kerrville. The location dictated one of the more unusual designs ever drafted for a medical facility.

The hospital would be built on Water Street between the corners of Sidney Baker and Earl Garrett streets, and across the street from where Boss had first begun his business career in the Weston Garage. Located at the ground floor corner was an eleven-pump Humble gasoline station. The first three floors were rented to retail and office space to provide the hospital an additional source of income. The fourth, fifth, and sixth floors would house a fifty-five-bed hospital and supporting medical staff.

The project took five years to come to fruition with the dedication of the hospital. Boss and Charlie had to pool almost $1 million to get it done, a staggering sum for a ranching community in those days.

Earlier on, at the July 5 trustees meeting held at Peterson's Garage and Auto Company in 1946, the Foundation had a total of $150,000 on deposit in the Chas. Schreiner Bank—far below the amount needed to build a hospital. To get the project completed, the Petersons had to be able to funnel money more directly into the Foundation. The Foundation would need to do business with the companies owned by the Petersons, and the Foundation wanted to buy land owned by the Petersons, so Boss and Charlie decided they should leave the board of their own Foundation.

At a special called meeting of the Hal and Charlie Peterson Foundation on November 13, 1946, Boss and Charlie resigned from the Foundation which carried their names. The minutes of this meeting read:

> The following trustees were present: C. H. Gilmer (an attorney from Rocksprings); W. A. Fawcett, Sr. (the Kerrville furniture store owner); W. Scott Schreiner; Guy G. Griggs . . . Guy G. Griggs, secretary-treasurer of the foundation, stated that in the absence of a president he would restate the purpose of this meeting and that it was for the election of president and vice president of the board to replace Hal Peterson and Charlie Peterson, recently resigned. On a motion by C. H. Gilmer and seconded by W. A. Fawcett Sr., W. Scott Schreiner was elected president by unanimous vote of the board to fill the unexpired term of Hal Peterson. On a motion by C. H. Gilmer and seconded by Guy G. Griggs, W. A. Fawcett, Sr., was elected vice president by unanimous vote of the board to fill the unexpired term of Charlie Peterson. . . .

Scott Schreiner, owner of the Schreiner Department Store in

downtown Kerrville and a member of the Schreiner family known throughout the Hill Country, proved a good choice to head the Foundation. Schreiner and Fawcett, the furniture store owner, were both outstanding operators of businesses, and certainly had the know-how to keep a struggling new hospital on the path to fiscal soundness.

This move cleared the way for solid progress to be made toward construction of the hospital. At the June 7, 1947, meeting of the Foundation board, the trustees restated the Foundation's goals as follows:

> First, the main objective of this Foundation is to establish a non profit hospital in the City of Kerrville for the benefit of the people of the Hill Country in general. Second, the aim of this Foundation is to perpetuate this hospital in the years to come by providing some sort of a continuous and lasting revenue.

At this watershed meeting, the trustees voted that the hospital should be placed in downtown Kerrville instead of on the outskirts of town. The board also required that "the building be erected with suitable space for rental purposes to create enough income to reasonably assure the hospital of a perpetual and lasting income."

The minutes of the meeting note:

> First, it was established that Petersons' Garage and Auto Company owned a piece of property on the corner of Water and Sidney Baker Streets, formerly occupied by the old St. Charles Hotel, and it was further established the Petersons' Garage and Auto Company had plans for a two-story building to be erected on this property and that the first floor was to be occupied by commercial business concerns and that the second floor would be rental office space. It was further established that Petersons' Garage and Auto Company would be willing to sell this property for the price paid by them ($40,000), plus the money expended by them for the contemplated building plans ($3,750).

From that moment, the hospital project progressed rapidly. Construction on the building's foundation began in 1947 and cost $81,560.

To open the process up more to the community leadership, the trustees met on July 7, 1947, and named a Hospital Advisory

Board. Original members named to this board were Milton Pampell, Dr. S. E. Thompson, W. R. Meredith, L. B. Brown, E. B. Carruth, Mrs. Scott Schreiner, Mrs. H. E. Butt, J. F. Stallings, J. G. Cox, and Mrs. W. A. Salter.

The purpose of the advisory committee was stated: "This committee is to study the plans of the hospital, to plan the equipment of the hospital, and to advise with the Board of Trustees on all matters pertaining to the management and administration of the hospital."

The architects objected strongly to Boss's concept that the hospital have retail space and a gasoline station underneath it. The "art of architecture" for such an imposing building would somehow be compromised by mixing it with such differing commercial ventures. Gasoline under a hospital? Surely no one had ever heard of such a thing, they argued.

But Boss insisted that the fledgling new hospital would need income to maintain such a building, and even though Boss was no longer on the Foundation's board, it surprised no one that his view prevailed. It was, after all, his money, his vision, his gift. And Charlie softly stood in support of his brother.

The major construction contract for the hospital was led at the January 15, 1948, meeting of the Foundation's board. By that time, the Foundation had received $687,987 in donations as follows:

Donations:	
Kerrville Bus Company, Inc.	
December 30, 1944	$ 41,750
January 2, 1946	$ 42,000
January 6, 1947	$250,000
June 6, 1947	$ 2,000
December 26, 1947	$250,000
Hal and Charlie Peterson	
December 30, 1944	$ 32,000
January 2, 1946	$ 34,266
January 6, 1947	$ 30,000
Petersons' Garage and Auto Co.	
December 1, 1947	$ 3,750

Hal Peterson November 14, 1944	$	100
Equipment fund: W. A. Fawcett Furniture Co. January 8, 1946	$	1,000
Miscellaneous revenue: Sale of dirt	$	1,121
Total receipts:		**$687,987**

Expenses included architect fees of $24,500, taxes of $324, organization expense of $16, legal expense of $100, office expense of $24, and outside auditing expense of $60.

The Peterson Foundation had net receipts of $558,084 and was ready to proceed with the construction of the hospital building. The minutes of the January 15, 1948, meeting read:

> . . . The president (at that time W. A. Fawcett), next, called for a general discussion of the building plans and progress, and at this point, Mr. A. E. Noonan, architect, was called in and read and explained the various bids and sub-bids that had been received. After due discussion concerning the bids and sub-bids, Mr. G. W. Mitchell, whose bid on the building was low, was asked to explain to the trustees the escalator clause in his bid. After much discussion concerning this escalator clause, motion was made by W. Scott Schreiner and seconded by Henry P. Burney and voted by the trustees to accept Mr. Mitchell's bid of $555,972 on the contract of the building and that he be allowed an extra $15,000 to take care of any additional cost of labor or materials that might incur during the course of the construction—thus, making the bid firm at $570,972.
>
> It was then agreed by Mr. G. W. Mitchell that he would reduce his bid by $16,000 which was his estimate on the painting and allow the trustees to award the painting contract separately to a local Kerrville concern, provided the Kerrville local concern's bid was $16,000 or less.

The latter phrase was no doubt added to the contract because Boss insisted that Kerrville firms be used whenever possible.

Although the Foundation was still struggling to raise the cash for the hospital, the trustees reflected Boss's concern for Kerrville through the insistence that local painters have a chance to bid. And during this time, they even donated $2,000 to the Methodist Church for improvements in the Methodist Camp in Kerrville and $2,000 to the Presbyterian Church Fund for improvements at Schreiner Institute (now College).

Even so, the Foundation's trustees had to borrow money from Schreiner Bank on November 1, 1948, to complete the building and equip the hospital. They borrowed $150,000 on a short-term note with interest 4.5 percent. The trustees also authorized a long-term note from some other lender for $225,000 to be repaid over fifteen years from the rental income and income from the Foundation.

While in most of his businesses Boss left the details to others, the construction of the hospital was an exception. At construction meetings every Monday morning, Boss would sit in, said architect Tommy Noonan.

> He wanted to be sure his money wasn't being wasted. He didn't spend his money freely, and he surely didn't throw it away. But on the other hand, he wanted quality. He would always joke in his wry manner that the construction contract was "*cost plus plenty*." If a workman was goofing off on the job, Boss would sure mention it to me. If I was goofing off, he would sure mention it to my dad.
>
> Boss was really quite a sensitive man, but once he made up his mind to do something, he did it. . . . Boss was highly energetic, almost to the point of being a little hyper. He tended to sit on the edge of his chair and lean forward. If there was any question, he would sure jump on it. If he had a point to make or if he disagreed with something, he could be very aggressive about it.
>
> As a young architect, I was in awe of Boss originally and was somewhat apprehensive. Later on, the relationship got to be much more friendly and warmer both ways. I had a high regard for him. . . . I would say his IQ was up over 150.
>
> Here again, Charlie was exactly the opposite. He was kind of laid back, but he paid attention. He took in the presentations or the conversation. Charlie was very calm and didn't express himself too much. He was seldom critical.

According to Noonan, Boss visited Scott and White Hospital in Temple to gather ideas. While the hospital was under construction, Boss went through some terrible health periods. Noonan recalled visiting Boss at home when boards were being placed under his mattress to reduce the crippling effects of the arthritis. A visit to the Mayo Clinic eventually provided some relief. Dr. Kopecky flew with Boss to Rochester, Minnesota, and Boss became one of the first people to receive a shot of the new drug cortisone, which gave Boss great limbering-up relief.

When Boss got back after resting up for several weeks, he saw how slowly the work was progressing on the hospital. Boss set a deadline for completion of July 2, a date workers thought was almost impossible to meet, but they met it. Boss was at the construction site almost every day, surveying the building while sitting in his wheelchair.

"By adding the force of his own enthusiasm and his tremendous confidence in the fact that it could and must be done, the feat has been practically accomplished," an article in the *Kerrville Mountain Sun* reported.

On March 30, 1948, the trustees voted to hire E. E. Martin as superintendent of the proposed Sid Peterson Memorial Hospital at a salary of $500 a month. Martin was given the authority to begin the purchase of equipment and supplies and the hiring of staff for the hospital.

By the third annual meeting of the Hal and Charlie Peterson Foundation Board of Trustees on July 2, 1948, Supterintendent Martin was able to report that two-thirds of the office space reserved for doctors had been rented and that 90 percent of the commercial and office space had been leased. He outlined the tentative plans for the operation of a drug store, a laboratory, and an X-ray department. Supplies and equipment worth almost $100,000 were purchased from bids submitted to the trustees, and the hospital's opening was assured.

As the formal opening of the new hospital neared, Hal and Charlie Peterson opened the Humble gasoline station on the ground floor underneath the six-story skyscraper hospital on May 14, 1949.

The filling station, owned by Petersons' Auto Company and Garage, had three islands and eleven pumps. Ten of the pumps contained gasoline, and one had diesel fuel. The pumps were in three separate service centers. Each center was a complete service unit with overhead water and air hoses.

But the most unusual aspect of the service station was the air conditioning tubes which could be inserted into the vehicles for cooling. Borrowing from the hospital's air conditioning system, the tubes extended through the interior ceiling of the building to the outside service island. The tube completely cooled off the car during the time it took to get serviced.

The ground floor also housed a Goodyear store that sold tires, auto parts, and Hotpoint refrigerators, stoves and appliances for farm and home.

On that May day, the Petersons tried and succeeded in setting the all-time record for gasoline sales from a single location.

J. M. Blansett, Humble's division sales manager, surveyed the driveway crowded with cars and said: "I think we've set the final all-time high for the state in opening-day gallonage. I just don't see how it will be possible for any other station in the state to pump more gasoline than we've sold today."

A Humble publication added:

> Blansett was referring to the new all-time high set recently during the opening day of Hal and Charlie Peterson's ultra modern service station and tire store on the corner of Water and Sidney Baker Streets in Kerrville. Driveways that were crowded nearly every minute of the day indicated that every motorist in Kerrville and the surrounding Hill Country must have waited until the station opened to come in for service. The tremendous volume of gasoline sold during the day indicated that most of the cars, trucks, and buses came in with nearly empty tanks.
>
> The new station occupies the ground floor of the Sid Peterson Memorial Hospital building which will be opened later. The various departments in the station take up a total of 13,282 square feet. . . . General manager of the station and tire store is Bill Hahn, who has been with the Petersons for twenty-six years. Willie Woods is supervisor of the station. Coleman Knox, who recently completed a Humble Charted Lubrication course, is in charge of the wash and lubrication departments which contain the most modern equipment available.
>
> Humble products are not new to Kerrville motorists who have been trading at Peterson's where Humble has been sold for years. The old building across the street from the new station will be changed over to a bus depot. At present, it is headquarters for an automobile agency and contains the offices of the Peterson Interests. The offices will be moved to the second floor of the new (hospital) building soon.

CHAPTER 10

The Grand Opening

THE HOT SUNDAY AFTERNOON of July 3, 1949, proved one of the most important dates in Texas Hill Country history.

On that sultry but sunny afternoon, some 4,000 people witnessed the grand opening and dedication of Sid Peterson Memorial Hospital in downtown Kerrville. They toured the new facility, complete with fifty-five hospital beds and six stories. Only a few finishing touches remained to be completed.

W. A. Fawcett, chairman of the Foundation's board of trustees, presided over the opening ceremonies, which focused on pioneer rancher Sid "Cap" Peterson, for whom the hospital was named. Fawcett introduced the Peterson family, including Mrs. Sid C. (Myrta) Peterson; Mr. and Mrs. Joe Sid Peterson and daughter, Miss Nora Joe; Mr. and Mrs. Charlie Peterson; and Hal Peterson.

Dr. Sam E. Thompson, the pioneer tuberculosis doctor who ran Thompson Sanitarium from 1917 to 1935 when it was sold to the state (and is where Kerrville V.A. Hospital is now located), presented a brief sketch of the life of Cap Peterson.

Then the Rev. William Logan, pastor of First Presbyterian Church, gave the principal address. The pastor said he spoke "not as an individual or a member of any organized group but as a representative of the people of the community who voice their appreciation for the gift, the magnitude of which is so great that it is difficult to comprehend."

According to a news story in the *Kerrville Mountain Sun*, the pastor noted that a vast amount of resources were required to build such a hospital, and this meant a sacrifice of personal desires and needs. He also charged those who heard his speech that "they, too, had a responsibility, and as this hospital towers so prominently in the very heart of the community, that it should be a constant challenge for each of us to a life of sympathy and service to our fellow men."

The *Kerrville Times* reported that bronze tablets at the hospital entrances explain that the institution was built by the Hal and Charlie Peterson Foundation, dedicated to humanity in the memory of the father, Sid C. Peterson.

All afternoon and late into the evening, people from all over South and West Texas toured the third, fourth, and fifth floors which were open for public inspection. The sixth floor was opened a few days later, with the first patients admitted later in the month.

The hospital's second floor was devoted to rental space occupied by an attorney and physicians' offices, an accounting firm, and a beauty salon.

A preview of the hospital had been given to the medical community on the previous day, and a reception had been held in the Green Room of the Bluebonnet Hotel to honor the doctors who had come from all over the state. It was a "big pot in the little pot" uptown affair for country Kerrville with Hal and Charlie Peterson serving as hosts to some 400 guests.

The *Times* article stated: "Mrs. Chas. Peterson wore a white pique cocktail dress, and Mrs. (Guy) Griggs a blue dotted swiss. Mrs. Sid Peterson chose black crepe, and Mrs. (Sam) Thompson a beige. Miss (Nora Joe) Peterson wore a beige afternoon dress. Gorgeous arrays of pink gladiolus were used at vantage points throughout the room. . . . On the cocktail table was a swan carved of ice, which held the shrimp cocktail in its back."

An exotic heliconia was even brought in from the Hawaiian Islands to accent the thousands of flowers and hundreds of plants at the hospital's opening.

In his keynote address, Pastor Logan said: "It is said that every great institution is the lengthening shadow of a man. And how the shadow of the late Sid Peterson, who knew and loved this county, would have eyes twinkling and the corners of his mouth quivering with pleasure at the thought that his sons would make this magnificent gesture in his memory."

One visitor suggested that this hospital was an excellent answer to the doctrine of Communism, or "share the wealth." How could it ever be built and equipped if the dollars had been doled out singly to the people of the area, and how much more useful is this unselfish gift of a healing place? The visitor is said to have wondered such things.

The success of the opening was an example of Boss's instinctive understanding of public relations. The hospital's opening made news all over Texas and, indeed, across the nation for the unusual nature of its founding and its design. The July 18, 1949, issue of *Time Magazine* featured a picture of the hospital with a cutline headlined "PATIENTS, PUMPS & PROTECTION" which read:

> This is the Sid Peterson Memorial Hospital at Kerrville, Tex. (pop. 10,000), dedicated last week during the town's annual rodeo. Its outstanding feature: built-in protection against deficits. Hal and Charlie Peterson, rancher brothers who gave $1,000,000 to build the 55-bed hospital in memory of their father, decided that a hospital ought to have some source of income other than its patients. Peterson Memorial has an 11-pump gasoline station (center) and three floors of office space rented at 20 cents a square foot. Tenants included an attorney and a beauty parlor. The Peterson brothers figure that their commercial sidelines will net about $2,500 a month—15 percent of the hospital's operating costs.

The hospital opened with a medical staff of fourteen doctors and a nursing and support staff of about thirty-five people. It had a maternity section, two major and one minor surgery rooms, laboratory and X-ray facilities, kitchen and cafeteria, a nurse's dormitory, a physical therapy section, and a roof garden with furniture, plantings, sunlight, and a "magnificent view of the Guadalupe River and the hills."

The grand opening brochure boasted: "Nothing has been left undone at Sid Peterson Memorial Hospital to make patients feel at home. The furniture is modern, convenient, cheerful. The rooms are decorated in gay colors that will do as much for the patient's state of mind as the doctor does for his ills. Special type windows allow increased visibility, greater amounts of sunlight. There is a special section for colored patients, too. Unique among hospital equipment is the inter-communication system which enables a bedridden patient to talk with the nurse. Sid Peterson Memorial Hospital ranks with the nation's finest."

Missing from all the hoopla was any real indication of Boss and Charlie's key role in making the hospital possible. The official focus quite naturally fell on the father, whose honored name the hospital carried. But it was the business acumen of Boss which made possible the gathering of wealth to finance such a project, and it was the desire of Boss to do something for Kerrville which kept the project alive for about a decade before the doors could officially be opened.

The ceremonies and news accounts seemed to list Joe Sid Peterson and family and Charlie Peterson and family before Hal "Boss" Peterson in rank. If Boss resented not being first among the equals, he never expressed it. Though the entire community may have realized that Boss Peterson was the driving force behind the Foundation, the town never seemed to express it that way publicly. The newspapers contained tribute advertisements to "Hal and Charlie," one of which was penned by Howard E. Butt, the South Texas grocery store magnate, who stated as follows:

> My sincerest congratulations to Hal and Charlie Peterson on the completion and opening of their hospital. The building and facilities are such that any city in our state could be justly proud.
>
> . . . It should be a source of great satisfaction and pride to Boss and Charlie that they have created an institution that will adequately serve the needs of the sick and suffering of the Hill Country for several generations.
>
> . . . Nothing less than a great love for their fellow man, their hometown, and for the memory of their father could have moved them to put a large portion of their life's work into creating and providing for the permanency of an institution dedicated to the service of the needs of the Hill Country.
>
> . . . Boss Peterson, as the head of the Peterson Interests, is respected far and wide for his brilliant ability, his tremendous energy, courage, resourcefulness, and creative thinking that have achieved such notable success. I wonder if the people of Kerrville fully appreciate the greatness of his character, his success, and his contribution to the life of the Hill Country.

For the opening, Frank Stanush of Beverly Studios helped with the publicity. He also painted the portraits of Hal and Charlie which still hang in the hospital lobby.

But not everyone was happy. A strain remained in the community between the new hospital and some doctors who had practiced at Secor Hospital.

"Without being critical of any of the doctors of that period," said architect Tommy Noonan, "there was certainly a group from the old Secor Hospital who didn't want the Peterson hospital to be built. I remember that Boss was somewhat indignant with that. I guess that really grated on a man of his type when he was sacrificing to do something and certainly had no interest other than the welfare of the community. He got a little bitter about some of these doctors, and that carried over to some extent in the early relationships."

Despite the great success of the hospital's opening, Boss did have one major regret about what occurred. Boss said that the biggest regret of his life was that he did not also name the hospital after his mother. If he had it to do over again, he had told friends, he would have named it the Sid *and* Myrta Peterson Memorial Hospital.

CHAPTER 11

A Gift to the Hill Country

IF ONE EVENT COULD be said to have sealed Kerrville's status as "Capital of the Texas Hill Country," that event must have been the opening of Sid Peterson Memorial Hospital.

In the last half of the twentieth century, a city's reputation often rested on the quality of its medical care, and Kerrville had gone from having almost nothing to having one of the best small hospitals in the country virtually overnight.

The imposing building with turquoise blue trim which dominated Kerrville's downtown above the cypress-lined Guadalupe River symbolized the town's coming of age and was a major factor in spurring the growth which is still occurring in Kerr County.

Although many citizens originally came to Kerrville for health reasons, hoping the fresh air would help rid them of tuberculosis, the city really did not have the medical facilities to support the kind of retirement boom which dominates the area's growth today.

Suddenly, Kerrville became a regional medical center with Sid Peterson Memorial, the Veteran's Administration Hospital built south of town near the original Peterson homestead, and the Kerrville State Hospital.

From the outset, Sid Peterson Memorial Hospital revealed that it was a facility run by people with a keen understanding of business. The hospital soon swelled with high occupancy rates and, despite the normal financial struggles of a new institution, managed to break even very quickly. By the end of 1950, the Foundation trustees were able to report that the hospital had revenues of $218,712 and a net of $6,326, despite $4,744 spent for the opening of the facility and charged off in 1950.

That first full operating year the hospital incurred bad debts of about $8,000, of which the hospital had to charge off $5,000, the City of Kerrville and Kerr County covering about $3,000.

In a letter to the board on February 2, 1951, Guy Griggs wrote:

> The amount of $1,235.60 we have charged off for our patients represents people that doctors have sent to the laboratory and X-ray for services and the accounts were not paid. This is one of the things that so far as I know cannot be controlled. For your further information, I will say that no person has ever presented themselves to this hospital that were not taken in regardless of their financial standing. . . .
>
> For your information, I would like to say that we receive many compliments each week from patients in our hospital and from the families of patients in our hospital concerning the care and treatment they receive here. I think this is the best indication possible that we are rendering a good service. I would like to say further that we are gradually reaching out further from Kerrville and getting patients from other towns and that, in turn, these people pass the word along which makes additional patients from other communities.

Following the resignation of E. E. Martin in the fall of 1950, the board appointed Walton S. Daniel as hospital administrator at the same $500 per month salary.

The Foundation board also discovered that the twenty cents per square foot being charged for the leased space did not cover the $53,902 operating expenses of the building as originally hoped, and mid-1952, the board raised the rent to twenty-five cents per square foot to cover the $12,894 building maintenance deficit.

Boss always dreamed of making the hospital the "Mayo Clinic of the South," and his dream almost came true in 1951 and 1952 when the hospital negotiated with the Mayo Clinic in Rochester, MN, for five doctors from the famous clinic to move to Kerrville. At the very least, the Mayo Clinic agreed to help Kerrville locate and secure the medical specialists needed to round out the hospital's staff.

Problems with the negotiations began when the five Mayo specialists who wanted to come to Kerrville overlapped somewhat with the hospital's current medical staff. Eventually, the group from the Mayo Clinic made a proposal to come to Kerrville, but the trustees of the Hal and Charlie Peterson Foundation wound up rejecting their offer. Guy Griggs explained in a letter to the Mayo Clinic on January 22, 1952, which stated:

> We are fully aware that your training and background would add a great deal of prestige and would no doubt attract additional people to our hospital. By the same reasoning, we feel that if your coming should not attract enough additional people, from an area not already served by our institution, but that you simply divided the services rendered by our present staff among five additional men, then our own group would suffer economically in the same proportion as your group.
>
> We have given a great deal of consideration and thought to the possibility of attracting additional people to our institution from areas not already served by us and have reached certain conclusions with respect to this possibility. First, the population of this part of Texas is very sparse. This is a ranching country and the blocks of land owned by or operated by one family average from four thousand to a possible fifty thousand acres. If this were a farming country, there would probably be one family to each one hundred to two hundred acres. You can, therefore, see that much greater distances have to be considered when a ranch population is involved.

The letter went on to point out the distances from Kerrville to larger Texas cities, such as Austin, San Antonio, Uvalde, and San Angelo. "It would be our opinion that we could not expect to draw from an area of over half these distances, which is now being served by us to some extent," Griggs wrote. And the five Mayo Clinic specialists would still not round out the Kerrville Hospital's needs, Griggs noted. "We would still be short a neuro-psychiatrist, an otolaryngologist, a dermatologist, an allergist and obstetrician. By increasing the size of our staff some 50 percent at this time, it would certainly be impossible to add these needed four or five men for many years to come, and our community would still be short of a complete service," Griggs wrote.

Thus, dreams of a "Mayo Clinic of the South" evaporated when hard business facts prevailed, and Sid Peterson Memorial Hospital settled into its role as a regional, not a national, facility. Most likely, Boss was not happy that his vision for a new Mayo Clinic-type hospital did not become reality, but by that time in his life, he certainly had grown accustomed to being restrained by the more practical business sense of his associates, especially Guy Griggs, who "looked after" the hospital and Foundation and the Kerrville Bus Company in particular.

In the first couple of years, the hospital had received a little more than a million dollars in contributions from the various Peterson business interests.

For the first twenty years, the hospital operated at a slight financial loss which was made up by the Hal and Charlie Peterson Foundation. In two decades, the total loss was $938,189. At the end of that period, the hospital's cost for each patient was $61.86 per day while the revenue was $54.77, or a loss of $7.09 per patient day. The financial deficit was absorbed by the Foundation, which had also invested almost $2.3 million in the hospital to provide health care for the Texas Hill Country. The number of admissions to the hospital had grown from 1,344 in 1950 to 3,265 in 1968, and the number of major operations performed had gone from 202 to 577. The hospital staff had grown to 145 employees, and the medical staff listed sixteen physicians and four dentists.

By 1954, the Foundation also had given more than $100,000 to support other educational, religious, and charitable groups, and in 1956 the Foundation established the Peterson Youth Service Program which furnished counseling service to young people and made available loans to young men and women who were trying to reach their potential. In a decade, the Foundation had helped sixty students attend college with loans totaling more than $50,000. Dr. Andrew Edington, president of Schreiner Institute, agreed to supervise the program, and local business and professional people were asked to volunteer for the counseling program.

Like almost everything that happened concerning Peterson Interests, the youth service program was the brainstorm of Hal "Boss" Peterson, who said: "Frequently, a private Foundation may render a service which cannot be provided through public funds. It is with real pleasure that I look forward to the many years of service which this program will render to the Hill Country."

Although not officially a part of the program, Schreiner Institute handled the testing of the youth who sought help with both counseling and financing their college education.

The hospital's first major remodeling project was completed by the end of 1963 when the first floor, which had been the gasoline station, was absorbed by the hospital for an X-ray laboratory, general offices, and medical records. This project cost $350,000.

The second major step came in 1968, when a new wing was added to the sixth floor to allow for another twenty hospital beds, and a shell was created for a seventh floor. The second project also converted space on other floors to hospital uses as the growth of the medical facility gradually absorbed the entire building. The second phase cost more than $1 million.

A four-floor annex was added to the hospital in 1986, with a shell for two more floors. The annex houses a drive-through for emergency room traffic, a new operating room suite including a recovery room with twelve beds, six operating rooms, and an additional forty-four beds. The 1980s expansion cost about $6 million, with the Foundation pledging $3 million. For the first time, the public was called on to assist in the fundraising, and the community raised a matching $3 million through a committee headed by L. D. Brinkman and James Avery.

By that time, the hospital had 114 beds with nearly 500 employees and a medical staff of forty-eight. The annual operating budget was more than $9 million.

If Boss and Charlie could have lived to see what the hospital would become, it would no doubt have pleased them. Attorney Joe Burkett remembered the Boss saying: "We figured if we made our money from the people here, we ought to give it back here."

It was a big deal when the Humble gas station promoted "air conditioning while you wait." Humble attendant A. C. "Hotsie" Klein pumps air conditioning into the car of a Kerrville resident at the opening of the Sid Peterson Memorial Hospital.

— Photo courtesy of Sid Peterson Memorial Hospital scrapbook

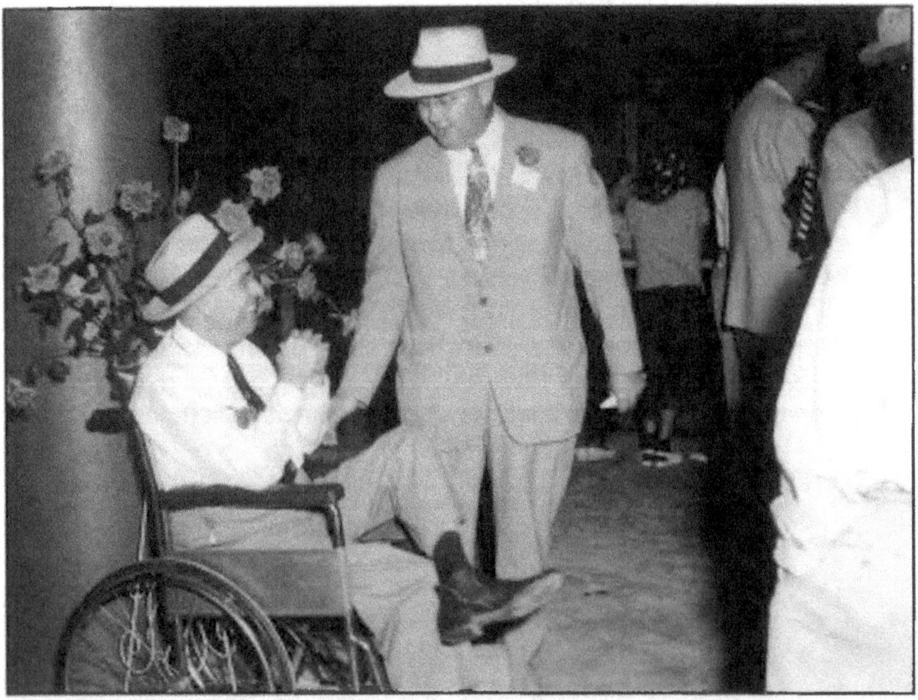

Boss Peterson (seated in wheelchair) greeting Frank Watts at the Sid Peterson Hospital opening day celebration.

— Photo courtesy of Sid Peterson Memorial Hospital scrapbook

The "Old" Secor Hospital formerly located on the corner of Sidney Baker and Main Street in Kerrville, Texas.
—Photo courtesy of Starr Bryden collection

Mr. and Mrs. Charlie (Violet) Peterson walking to the podium at the Sid Peterson Memorial grand opening ceremony. Seated from left to right is Nora Joe Peterson (brother Joe Sid's daughter) and Mrs. Sid Peterson (Hal and Charlie Peterson's mother).
— Photo courtesy of Sid Peterson Memorial Hospital scrapbook

Below: *1956 photo of downtown Kerrville, Texas, facing northwest, was taken from the roof top of the former Bluebonnet Hotel. Sid Peterson Memorial Hospital (tallest building) is visible in background on the right.*
— Photo courtesy of Starr Bryden collection

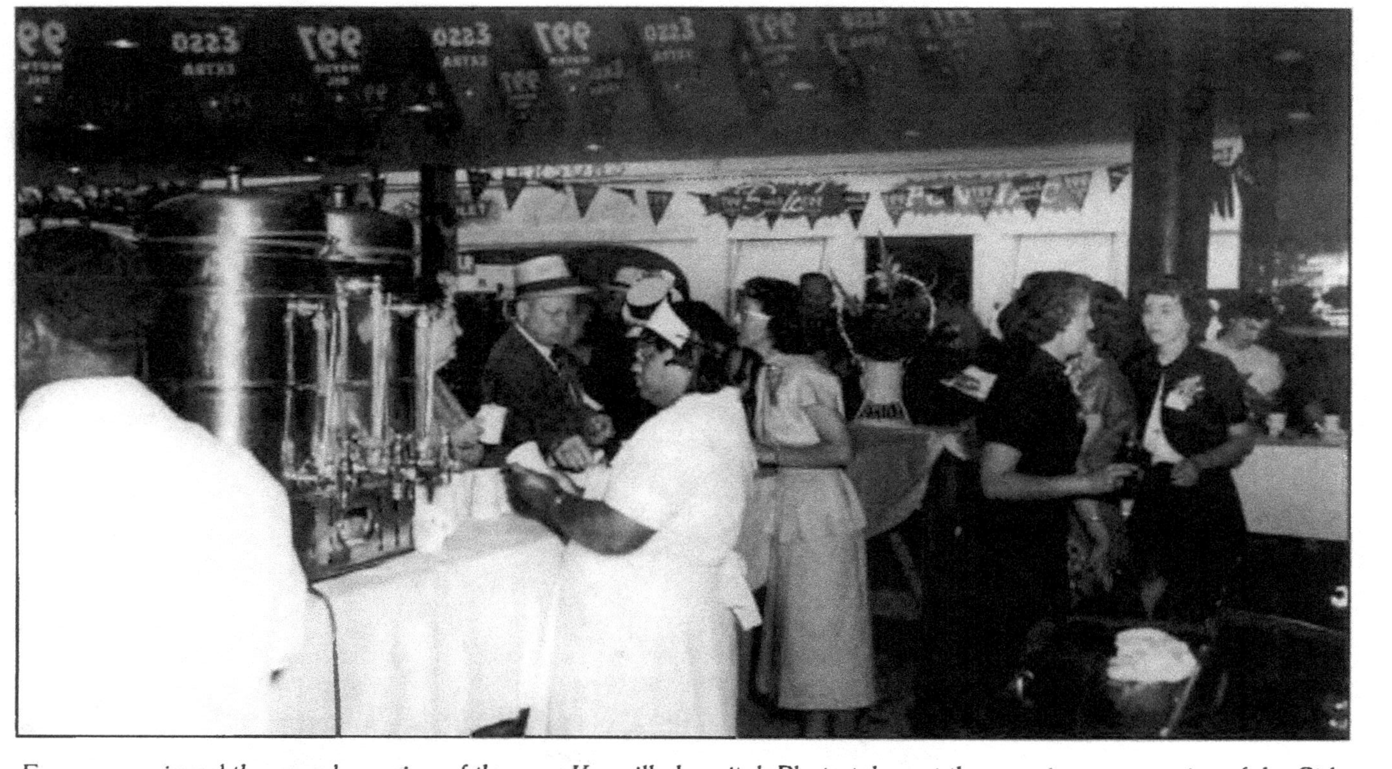

Everyone enjoyed the grand opening of the new Kerrville hospital. Photo taken at the opening ceremonies of the Sid Peterson Memorial Hospital. On the left in white coat is R.S.T. Walker helping to serve and on the right is Ruth Dempsey, holding soda bottle and talking with Mrs. Charlie (Josephine) Johnston.

— Photo courtesy of Sid Peterson Memorial Hospital scrapbook

Photo taken at the Sid Peterson Memorial Hospital opening day celebration. On far left is Hal and Charlie Peterson's "Lieutenant" Guy Griggs. Charlie Peterson is standing third from the left.

— Photo courtesy of Sid Peterson Memorial Hospital scrapbook

Sid Peterson Memorial Hospital photo taken during the 1950s.
The Humble gas station and retail stores were located "below" the hospital.

—Photo courtesy of Dr. Rector

Right: *Brass plaque that hangs in the Sid Peterson Memorial Hospital named in honor of Hal and Charlie Peterson's father Sid "Cap" Peterson.*

Below: *The Sid Peterson Memorial Hospital Medical Staff in the 1950s. Front row, left to right: Dr. Duan Packard, Dr. Charles Jones, Jr., Dr. Hugh Drane, Dr. Earl Gregg. Back row, left to right: Dr. Dan Bacon, Dr. Barney Williams, Dr. William Byrd, Dr. Choice Matthews.*

PART FOUR

The Land

View of the land before the "park that was built in a day" was constructed.

CHAPTER 12

Unveiling Heaven

WHEN TEXANS PICTURE HEAVEN, they think of the Hill Country, the part of the state that "God got right."

That seems to be particularly true of Texans from the Houston area. For a reason that no one can fully explain, there has always been a love affair between the Houston area and Kerrville.

Walk down the streets of Houston and ask the residents where they would prefer to be, and most will reply: the Texas Hill Country, near Kerrville. Perhaps living in the heat and humidity allows coastal dwellers to more fully appreciate the dry and slightly higher altitudes of the inland hills because Houstonians have long made Kerr County a second home. A surprising number of the students at Schreiner College have always come from the Houston area, and so do many of those who attend the many exclusive summer camps which dot the Kerrville hills. One can still hear the natives call a stretch of the Guadalupe River above Kerrville by the nickname "Houston Row" because so many of the houses were occupied by people who currently lived in or had retired from the Bayou City. The big city residents have contributed mightily through projects such as the incredible Hill Country Arts Foundation, and they have prevented Kerrville from being the tightly bound ranching community it might have been and forced it to be the more cosmopolitan area it is today.

However, the Texas Hill Country had not yet been discovered in the early days of Boss Peterson. Through his business entertaining, Boss helped to unveil the hills.

Boss learned that he could do business if he could get people to enter his ranching heritage. In 1940 he and Charlie bought Camp Eagle, a 6,465-acre ranch on the Hackberry prong of the Nueces River which rushes through the Hill Country before meandering its way down to the Gulf of Mexico at Corpus Christi. Four dams on the ranch captured water from the Hill Country springs. The main cabin featured a kitchen and bar with a flower-decked veranda which overlooked the crystal main lake of the ranch. Guests stayed in cabins made of native limestone which would house eight people each. Camp Eagle also had a heated swimming pool, unusual for its day. Camp Eagle was dedicated to the "pleasure and fellowship of friends and business associates."

Boss spent as much time at Camp Eagle as possible, but Charlie rarely took part in the entertaining. Charlie sought private refuge at his HiLo hunting cabin on the Peterson Stock Farm east of Kerrville, where he played cards with close friends and spent time with family.

Although Camp Eagle was always a working ranch, Boss was one of the first to see the potential of Camp Eagle and other hunting ranches in Texas. The native deer and game birds provided excellent hunting, and Boss supplemented them by turning Camp Eagle into one of the first exotic game preserves. Boss was among the first to bring the exotics to Texas ranches, and he was the first to install the tall game fences so common in the Texas Hill Country today.

Boss stocked antelope, buffalo, axis deer, Texas longhorns, elk, aoudad and mouflon mountain sheep, and other smaller game. He directed his loyal Camp Eagle ranch foreman, Marion Smith, to conduct breeding experiments with a number of different kinds of antelopes, and he also stocked various types of fish in ponds on his land. Boss was the first person to lease the famed YO Ranch west of Kerrville for business hunting purposes, an action which paved the way for what is today a major Hill Country industry.

Stepdaughter Betty Lee Halff remembers a Camp Eagle story when Boss struggled to make a tough decision. "Boss was a great patron of animals, which was one of the many things that I admired about him. I also admired his sense of right and wrong. One dilemma I recall was when an eagle was killing his sheep." Boss was on the Fish and Game Commission at the time, and eagles were on the endangered species list. "He felt it wasn't right that a predator was killing his lambs. Knowing that he would face criticism, he went ahead and had the eagle killed. He got a call from one of the game wardens who said, 'Boss, you can't do that.' But he did. Boss lived his life as he saw it. He was not tortured in any way by public opinion."

One story suggests Boss's control of his hunting parties. When Beck, a bus manufacturing partner from Ohio, came down to hunt, Beck shot deer from cars and pickups. Boss and Beck came across a nice buck, and it was Beck's time to shoot. Boss made Beck get out of the car, load his gun, but then Boss said, "Wait, wait, let him get a little closer" two or three times. When the buck got close enough, Boss shot it without getting out of the car. His explanation was, "Beck, you didn't have any business killing a deer that good."

Being frail, Boss rarely hunted, leaving that up to his brothers, his associates, and his guests. He seemed to have little interest in the hunt personally. Perhaps he was limited by his health, but he gained more "trophies" sitting around the table in the main cabin where he spun yarns and drank heavily into the early hours of the following day. Or he played the organ for practice or for guests. Business was not discussed formally while guests were at Camp Eagle; however, the foundation of friendship and trust was poured and set, so the deals could be constructed quickly the following week. Boss viewed the hunting weekends as part of a "softening-up process."

Frank Stanush, the official photographer for many of the hunting trips, said, "Of course, Beverly Studios did all the photos at Camp Eagle. Boss had me taking pictures of the big executives with their hunting trophies and as a courtesy we sent them the pictures."

Although Boss and Charlie rented Camp Eagle to outside people and organizations and often used it for family purposes, the clear principal function of Camp Eagle was entertaining for Peterson Interests. In its heyday, most weekends found Boss being driven up from San Antonio with a group of General Motors executives out of Detroit, politicians from local councilmen to governors, or bankers or business associates from almost everywhere. Some of the most famous names in Texas and the nation passed through Camp Eagle in the 1940s and 1950s.

It is said that when some of the locals gave directions to the party ranch, they would say, "Just follow the whiskey bottles to Camp Eagle."

Secretary Willa Mae said the hunting trips were very costly: "The liquor bill was the main thing, and Boss always had to have extra help. But Boss did claim them as a business expense . . . every one of them. The Internal Revenue Service came back on him and threw out a lot of them. When the auditors came to the office, I had to dig out all those bills and guests logs. They went over every one of them and wanted to know who was hunting at the time."

Few people who passed through Camp Eagle could ever forget the most famous feature of the ranch: R. S. T. "Rastus" Walker, the short black man who was Boss's driver and Man-Friday for two decades. Close associates don't remember seeing Boss drive, but they all remember Rastus behind the wheel of the Oldsmobile station wagons that Boss loved.

Rastus tended bar and took care of all the guests' needs. He was a great cook who put guests to bed after the poker game at 2:00 A.M. and got them up at 4:00 A.M. to go deer hunting.

Veteran Kerrville businessman Carl Meek noted: "It didn't take long to spend the night at Camp Eagle."

But more importantly, Rastus entertained anyone who came near him. He could sing like the Ink Spots and tell the funniest stories with impeccable timing. He delivered lunches to the hunters, kept their spirits up both literally and figuratively, and tended to any needs visitors expressed. By nature, Rastus was a hustler and a promoter, a "pistol" in the cowboy vernacular, and some called him the unofficial mayor of "the settlement," the black neighborhood of Kerrville.

Rastus was Boss's constant companion from San Antonio to Kerrville to Camp Eagle.

Rastus not only drove Boss, but he was his valet as well. He took care of all of Boss's personal needs during the years when Boss was not married, and he had the run of the houses. One Saturday night, Boss discovered that all of his whiskey had been consumed by Rastus, and with anger Boss fired Rastus. But the "morning rule" prevailed, and Boss hired him back on Monday.

Good credit was very important to Boss, and he was said to advise that if you borrow on a thirty-day note, pay it back in twenty-nine days to keep your good credit rating. He was proud that people said, "If a Peterson says he'll pay, he'll pay."

But Rastus loved putting the touch on people, and he tried to borrow money from the guests at Camp Eagle. Boss would warn his visitors not to lend Rastus money, but the warning was no antidote to his employee's silver tongue. Rastus probably talked most of the guests out of at least a little cash. Boss often discovered later, much to his dismay, that Rastus had charmed a wealthy business associate out of a "hundred-dollar loan" on the ride to the airport. "Rastus gave Boss a lot of trouble," said Frank Stanush, "but he was worth it."

One story goes that a banker came to Boss and informed him that Rastus wanted to borrow $600. The banker said he would loan Rastus the $600 if Boss would co-sign the note. Boss replied to the banker, "If you'll co-sign the note, I'll lend Rastus the $600 myself."

Recalled Mrs. Garland "Snookie" Scogin, an employee of Peterson Auto Company: "They threw away the mold when they made Rastus. He was very polite. He would bow and scrape, take off his hat, and bow down when he came into the office to pick up his check."

Boss's stepdaughter, Betty Lee Halff said, "Rastus played his relationship with Boss like an old fashioned minstrel. Superficially it was Boss and servant. It was part of his show to behave in the old fashioned way and say 'yassah, yassah.' He was an actor.

"Many times Rastus would have to help Boss when he was sick and lift him into bed. He looked after Boss like a man servant would, and there was a lot of mutual respect between them, certainly a great deal of affection.

"And then he (Rastus) had all these other attributes, like singing and dancing, making jokes and responding to people in ways that African-Americans used to in the early days. They don't do that anymore, and we don't expect them to."

Tom Syfan recalled that "Boss gave Rastus a lot of jiving and fun, and Rastus would play right back. They had a lot of fun together. Boss rode Rastus pretty hard, and Rastus accepted it . . . and the money that came along with it."

Secretary Willa Mae commented that all the well-to-do families wanted to hire Rastus because he could run things. "But Rastus loved Mr. Peterson. Rastus always bought things and charged them to Boss. That was what he was supposed to do, and he did it. He signed slips of paper, and that was all that was necessary. I really think that no matter what Mr. Peterson had of value, he would have trusted it to Rastus because he was very loyal and Rastus took care of him when he was sick."

Rastus stayed with Boss, mostly living in a small servant house in the back. After Boss married Billie in 1954, things changed. Billie looked after Boss in ways Rastus never could, and she stabilized his lifestyle, probably adding years to his life. Billie, not an extravagant person, naturally resented that Rastus thought he had free rein to everything that involved Boss, and she once put a lock on the refrigerator door to keep Rastus out.

Billie said she had to lock the refrigerator because Rastus would go to town loaded down with food for all his friends.

"Rastus didn't like me because he knew Boss was so devoted to me, but I never got between those two. Boss fired him twice. I rehired him before he got to the highway because there was something special there between those two," Billie said.

Billie's daughter, Betty Lee, remembers her mother fussing about Rastus. "Boss needed Rastus for physical purposes, but I think there was also another kind of affinity there that went way back. I'm sure before mother came along there wasn't much surveillance . . . there were times that there were confrontations, and I'm not sure that mother won. I think most of the time she lost, but she dealt with it gracefully."

Everyone who was associated with the Petersons remembers the long and loyal relationship between Boss and Rastus.

"Rastus was an extension of Uncle Boss," said Beverly Sullivan, Charlie's stepdaughter. "Because of that, he played a big role in our family too. I remember him chauffeuring me to school in a big Cadillac wearing his uniform, and when we got there, he would get out of the car and open my door for me."

Rastus was forty-five years old when Boss died. Rastus married while Boss was alive but later divorced. After Boss died, various people who had been entertained at the hunting camps hired Rastus and paid him quite well, but Rastus was never very happy. With Boss, Rastus had a carefree life, and Rastus didn't like to be tied down in one place. Rastus wound up working for the owner of a Houston General Motors dealership.

During the 1980s, shortly before Rastus died, Boss's cousin, Dash Peterson, ran into him on a Kerrville street. Dash recalls hollering out to Rastus to grab his attention. Times had changed and an older Rastus turned around and warmly but firmly stated, "Mr. Peterson, my name is R. S. T. Walker. It never was Rastus."

Billie became an intricate part of the entertaining that Boss did frequently at Camp Eagle. She could play the organ and sing, and she added a hostess quality to rustic Camp Eagle which allowed Boss's entertaining hunting parties to be even more effective for business. Betty Lee Halff said, "Mother completed Boss in a way that he was not able to do for himself. He was not a natural host but he certainly had hospitable inclinations. During the hunting season when they had large parties, mother was in her prime. She was always there to meet and greet and make sure the guests had plenty to eat."

"Boss did good when he married Billie," said attorney Joe Burkett. "She was a real soldier."

Beverly Sullivan recalled those occasions: "Billie was very charming and warm. She could have been anything from a general's wife to a president's wife because she was very personable, outgoing, and gracious. She was a nice person to be at Uncle Boss's side in those later years."

Boss knew the importance of making sure city people understood something about hunting. Once when an unfavorable report appeared on the front page of a Houston newspaper, Boss invited a number of the newspaper's editors and top reporters to see a hunt and learn why it was good for Texas. His plan worked, and the newspaper ran another front-page story which emphasized the positive aspects.

Boss also insisted that ranches not be cut off from the community. In the 1930s when Boss entertained and "did business deals" at his Diamond Bar Ranch, he demanded—and became the first person in the county to obtain—a private telephone line, even though it required that a phone cable be extended from Rocksprings out to the Diamond Bar Ranch, a distance of ten miles.

At Camp Eagle, Boss was forced to share a party line, which he hated. When he began to talk business over the telephone and wanted privacy, Boss began swearing to clear the line of unwanted ears. Then he would listen for all the clicks.

Although early in life Boss had served on some local governmental boards in Kerrville, his political life was limited to helping launch other careers, such as Claud Gilmer's and Joe Burkett's service as state representatives. The only foray Boss made into state politics came in 1954, when he was appointed by Governor Allan Shivers to the Texas Game and Fish Commission.

The *San Antonio News* heralded his appointment as follows:

> Though a bona-fide resident of San Antonio for several years, Peterson actually is a Kerrville man, famed there as a business tycoon, rancher and a devoted conservationist of turkey and deer. No man in this area can equal his great practical knowledge of the habits of the Hill Country's most popular game and bird animals.

The *San Antonio Light* noted that Boss had for thirty years been one of the Southwest's foremost conservationists, and added:

> Peterson impresses us as a man who likes to do an outstanding job on anything he undertakes. We know he's been a part of the long-time program in the ranch country that brought the Virginia white-tail from a point close to extinction to its current place as the state's No. 1 game animal, increasing annually over a wide area despite the pressures of heavy hunting. We know for sure he treasures a reputation as a fine sportsman.

While on the commission, Boss experimented with wild game, particularly a genetic project designed to make Hill Country deer grow bigger antlers. Boss served a number of years on the commission despite his failing health and hectic business schedule. No doubt, he found the energy and time to do so because of his passion for wildlife and his vision of what hunting and exotics would come to mean for the Hill Country.

CHAPTER 13

An Impulsive Legend

FOR A MAN WHO thought about business constantly for twenty-four hours a day, nothing was too impulsive for Boss Peterson, especially when he was imbibing in a little strong drink—which was most afternoons and virtually every night.

In 1938, Boss was admiring his first air-conditioned bus and got an idea to set out on a road trip.

"Let's go to California," he blurted out, and they did. Unfortunately, the air conditioning went out in the desert halfway there.

But the most impulsive period came when Boss had his own airplane, a seven-seat, twin-engine Beechcraft, and he kept pilot Junior Fawcett standing by. Junior, who had learned to fly with the British Royal Air Force and the U.S. Army, flew Boss to meetings all over the country from New York to California.

An effort to fly to New Orleans, however, cooled Boss's passion to go against the elements. Junior advised Boss that the weather was too heavy to travel by air to New Orleans, but Junior was unable to make Boss understand. Boss had been drinking and insisted on trying. Following a rough trip from Kerrville to Houston, Boss and Junior were stranded for a day by the bad weather. Boss called his chauffeur Rastus and made Rastus drive to Houston to pick him up. Boss returned to Kerrville by automobile.

About this time, the Petersons enacted the "middle of the

night" rule. Junior could fly Boss anywhere he wanted to go in the morning, but the pilot was to remain grounded for any flights Boss insisted on taking in the middle of the night.

"Don't take me on that airplane in the middle of the night," Boss told Junior, "even if I demand that you fly me somewhere. I may fire you that night, but don't worry. I'll hire you back in the morning."

The "middle of the night" rule applied not only to firings and airplane flights but also to decisions made after midnight. Everyone understood it wasn't a decision unless Boss made the same one the following morning.

"Some people accused Boss of being drunk too much," an associate said. "Maybe so, but Boss had more sense drunk than most people do cold sober."

Dick Staudt, who managed the tire testing fleet, said he received a call from Charlie Johnston one afternoon to drive Boss and a lady friend to Dallas. Along the way, Staudt said Boss told a story about a previous trip to Dallas. Boss said he and a friend had left a downtown party and were searching for a ride to their hotel. The two had been drinking heavily, and all they could find was a milk truck, which they "borrowed" to drive to the hotel. The joyride resulted in another ride for Boss to the Dallas jail.

Boss had a "beautiful office" on the second floor of the hospital, but the staff estimated that he only came down to it about one day a month.

"Then it would take the rest of the month to straighten out the trouble he caused on that one day," secretary Willa Mae laughed.

Charlie stayed at the office even less. He was rarely there unless Boss insisted he come to a meeting.

Joe Burkett moved to Kerrville to start his law practice after digging ditches to earn his way through school. He quickly learned of the legendary Boss Peterson, as he handled minor legal matters for Peterson's Garage and Auto. "I was just a country lawyer who represented those who wanted to hire me. As a country lawyer, I didn't meddle in anybody's business unless they asked me."

But one day, Burkett recalled that Boss wanted to see him. Boss had a petroleum transport company and was hauling fuel from the refinery to the military with twenty-two trucks. Boss had a "hat full of money" at that time, but he was trying to do a transaction with a Houston bank involving $2.2 million, an unbelievable amount of money, and the young attorney was cautious about giving legal advice involving such a sum.

Boss tossed the $2.2 million note to Burkett and asked for an opinion. Burkett read the contract and pointed out a couple of problems, and Boss added: "It don't look worth a damn to me."

Boss had Burkett call the bank and simply say: "Change it, or we'll find another bank."

Burkett did and thought he had just queered that business deal, but Burkett said he had no sooner hung up the telephone than the bank called back to make the changes Boss wanted.

Burkett, later elected as state representative from Kerrville with a landslide eleven-vote margin, continued to do some legal work for the Petersons, but Boss's main attorney was R. N. "Skinny" Gresham from San Antonio.

Boss was an area distributor for Humble Oil and Refining Company, which he had Charlie Dempsey "looking after." He had ownership or stock in a number of banks, real estate, and land, including a pecan company in San Angelo. He had ownership in Modern Builders, Products Lumber and Supply, Lone Star Beer Distribution Company in Lubbock, Halbart Company, Yellow Cab Company of Kerrville, West Texas Auto Company, Beverly Studio, Castle Investment Corp., KERV Radio, American Pure Milk, Schreiners Wool and Mohair, Texas Consolidated Transport Company, the Worldwide Mapping Company, and many more firms that he bought in and sold out of in shorter periods of time.

Because they were almost always partners, the silent partner Charlie had an equal interest in whatever Boss did.

Charlie rarely appeared to be an active partner with Boss, whom the cowboys believed could "out drink and out trade" anybody in the state. Boss had a way of getting people to do what he wanted them to do.

Charlie was, as the ranch hands said, "a little light for that kind of hauling." But Charlie shared his father's taste for poker and his brother Joe Sid's love of the outdoor life. He could fit right in around the campfire where the cowboys "tell the biggest lies you ever heard in the world."

Cousin Dash Peterson remembered the quiet afternoons when Charlie would take him down to the river to cook over an open fire.

Charlie lived an orderly life of visiting with people up and down the streets of Kerrville in the mornings, hunting or fishing in the afternoon, and parties with family and friends at night. After he married and settled down, he tended his yard and garden.

"Charlie had a great big garden, and he was so proud of it even though it was Joe Pruneda who did most of the work," Beverly Sullivan said. "But Charlie would brag on the tomatoes like they were his. I remember him in the kitchen making homemade chow-chow, which was about the extent of his domestic capabilities."

While he and Joe Sid shared a love of outdoors, Charlie did not have his brother's wild side. Joe Sid would often say: "I've spilled more whiskey than that before breakfast," and he wasn't joking. Joe Sid was known to carry sheep in the back seat of his Cadillac and let them out on the streets if it suited him.

Boss, too, had his weaknesses, but those did not diminish his stature.

"Boss was a great man," said Clyde Parker, Kerrville businessman. "He had certain faults, but he left a tremendous legacy."

While brothers Charlie and Joe Sid spent more time outdoors than Boss could do or cared to do, Boss kept his ties to his ranching heritage. There was a time in Boss's life when he "loved to can food in order to relax."

Mary Hutto recalled that Boss adored new ideas and gadgets. She remembered a time when Boss came to her mother's house with a new apparatus for canning under his arm. "Mrs. Hyde," Boss said, "you don't need to can with jars anymore; you use cans." Boss brought along bushels of tomatoes and spent the morning helping her mother learn the new canning method. After they were finished, Boss gave the canning to her mother.

"That was his way of getting his mind off big business and relaxing," said Mary Hutto. "He would can everything he could get his hands on."

Boss's stepdaughter Betty Lee said, "When Boss had something that he liked, he wanted everybody to have one. I remember the year that he found out about the Have-A-Heart animal traps, an invention that captures animals without maiming or killing them. He made sure all of his friends had those traps. It was the same way with Cool Vent Umbrellas. They were made in the 1950s and beautifully constructed and perfect for poolside. The wind goes through special vents in the umbrella and prevents the umbrella from blowing over. Boss had to have one and he bought one for all his friends with pools. He always wanted to share the happiness and he was able to do it."

Ben Hyde, Sr., who worked a variety of jobs for Boss, once was a test driver for West Texas Auto Company. Later he worked on the Peterson ranches and often bought and sold horses for Boss.

"One thing about Boss, he never told me what to do or what not to do," Hyde said. "Boss wanted me to deliver these horses to a man in Ohio, but he never told me the price he wanted for them. I had to figure it out for myself."

Boss trusted him because Hyde had traded with his father, Mister Sid. It once took Hyde two days to sell the contrary Mister Sid a barn-load of hay for $14, more than double what Hyde had paid for it.

"The Petersons didn't pay a whole lot," Hyde said, "but they gave you all the help you needed. If the job took five men, they might give you ten."

Although Boss didn't ride, he inherited his father's love for horses, and the Peterson Stock Farm and ranches raised some of the best in South Texas. They were perhaps best known for their golden palominos, although they also raised quarter horses and Tennessee walking horses.

A brochure for the Diamond Bar Ranch pitched the horses in this way:

> The Diamond Bar Ranch is the home of some of the most beautiful golden palomino horses in the entire Southwest. They are ranch-raised high on the healthful Edward's Plateau where soundness and hardiness become part of their many good traits.

Their number-one stallion, Pleasant King, was grand champion stallion at the Fort Worth Stock Show in 1940 and won many other ribbons and cups as a show horse. Pleasant King was also featured wearing his silver saddle in a Lone Star Beer ad that was displayed in bars all over Texas. A bay stallion called Rocky was grand champion at the Stamford Cowboy Roundup and Rodeo in 1944, winning against the King Ranch's best horse, Hired Hand.

"The palomino horses were all the rage in those days," said Frank Stanush. "They brought about $5,000 each. Pleasant King was in a Lone Star Beer advertisement with my wife, Dorothy, standing next to the horse. It was in every bar in San Antonio."

The Peterson ranches also raised Hereford cattle, Corriedale and Suffolk sheep, toy Shetland ponies, Angora goats, and Border collies, which became a particular passion for Boss.

Tom Syfan, one of Boss's Border collie trainers, first visited the Peterson ranch in the early 1940s. Syfan had a dog that would work, and he wanted to breed her with one of the Peterson Border collies. However, Boss would not allow it because Syfan's dog was not purebred Border collie. But Syfan got to know Street Hamilton, who was running the Peterson ranches, including the Peterson Stock Farm. At that time, the Border Collie Association would not register puppies for reproduction until they were certified as working dogs. Street hired Syfan to train the dogs to the level required for certification.

The Petersons' Diamond Bar Ranch participated in many sheep dog trials and had many champions. Boss headed a committee to form the first Southwestern Sheep Dog Trials, even putting in a division for "Texas Range Dogs" for ranchers who felt their dogs were top performers but without the strict discipline of the regular trials. "Rooster was one of Boss' most famous Border collies and could work in Spanish and English," Syfan said.

The Diamond Bar Ranch touted the Border collies as "wonderful pets for children and the smartest, most alert dog alive." But mostly, the dogs were useful in handling livestock. A 1940s brochure from the Diamond Bar Ranch read:

> In these days of an abundance of work and critical labor shortage, border collie sheep dogs can be taught to do the work of two men, horses, and then some! Ranchers who own and work these dogs consider them priceless. Over a period of years, one dog will save hundreds of dollars in labor costs. Ask any rancher who owns one.
>
> The border collie sheep dog was imported from Scotland, where for centuries his ancestors used to work livestock on the Scottish border. He stands about 16 to 19 inches high at the shoulders and has a heavy silken coat, which is usually black with white markings although some individuals have a little tan.
>
> His disposition is gentle and lovable. He is intelligent, obedient and easily trained. Border collies can be taught to watch,

drive, round up, cut out and catch sheep, goats, cattle, horses, hogs and even chickens and other barnyard fowl.

Border collies can "hold" livestock by fixing their eyes on the animals and bunching or driving them when necessary, penning them upon command.

Syfan told this story:

> I had a dog named Dasher and Joe Sid wanted to buy that dog. I remember one time when we were in the play room up at Camp Eagle. Boss and Joe Sid were sitting around this big, round oak table in front of the fireplace. Joe Sid was dickering with me about that dog. He had a roll of bills in his hand, green money, and he was rolling it like a pencil. I wanted $300 for that dog, which was a lot of money to me at that time. It probably wasn't anything to Joe Sid at all, but I was broke. Joe Sid was sitting straight across the table from me, and he rolled that roll of bills at me. I picked it up and counted $150. I didn't even look at him, and I rolled it back. That tickled Boss. I mean, he got a big charge out of that. It was the highlight of the weekend. Later, Boss came up to me and said, "Tom, come over here. I want to talk to you." He put his arm around my shoulder and said, "You treated Joe Sid just like he deserved." We were walking over to the horse corral, and when we got there, Boss pointed to a two-year-old horse and said, "Put that horse in your trailer and take him on home." He was half quarter horse and half walking horse. I named him Hal and rode him for ten or fifteen years. Later, I sold Dasher to Joe Sid for $300.

But the fun-loving Joe Sid had his ways to get even. When Syfan very cautiously nudged open the bump gate at Camp Eagle so it wouldn't hit the trailer, Joe Sid came barreling past him at forty miles an hour.

Syfan said he remembered one bit of advice from Boss for his entire sales life. Boss had told Syfan: "Now, Tommy, if a man flies a twin-engine airplane from California, don't sell him a $50 puppy. If you sell him a $50 puppy, he will wonder all the way back to California if that puppy was good enough. But if you sell him that same puppy for $500, he will damned well know he's good enough."

"Boss loved the sheep dogs," said Syfan. "His horses, his Border collies, and his exotic game were his hobbies. He didn't do it for the money. I doubt if there was any year that he broke even on the Border collies."

This love probably came because it gave the man, weakened by a bad heart and health problems, a continued tie to his ranching heritage. It gave him a reason to keep coming back to Kerrville and the land.

CHAPTER 14

Goodbye, Charlie

IN 1952, CHARLIE PETERSON'S heart began to fail.

After being ill for several months, his condition improved, and on a Sunday after Christmas, he visited the farm in the afternoon. On the following Monday, however, he fell ill again at noon. He died at about 3:00 P.M. Monday, December 28, 1953, at the age of fifty-two.

Violet's daughter, Beverly, remembers that she was viewing a movie at the Arcadia Theater when Charlie died. Charlie's mother came down to get her.

In Charlie's obituary, the *Kerrville Mountain Sun* noted:

> During the last few years, when ordered by his physician to take life a little more easily, he spent much of his time landscaping the grounds at his home and in his flower garden. Some of his flowers and shrubs were of the exhibition type, and he was quite proud of the results. He would not be in town for days at a time, and it is difficult for people to realize the kindly and sincere Charlie Peterson is no more.

Charlie's death provided the first glimpse that the two Peterson brothers were going to leave the vast part of their wealth to the Hal and Charlie Peterson Foundation. When Charlie's last will and testament was read, Charlie left to his widow, Violet Peterson, only one-half of the community estate existing between Charlie and Violet.

Most of Charlie's estate consisted of his separate property, but there was a smaller estate held "together" with his wife. Violet got the lavish modern house which she and Charlie had built a few years before he died, but she received no part of the Peterson Stock Farm in Kerr County, the Taylor Ranch in Edwards County, or Camp Eagle in Real County. Violet also received $100,000 in cash. The will established a monthly income of $1,500 for Violet, but she was to receive this money only as long as she remained unmarried. The will also set up an estate of $50,000 for his stepdaughter, Beverly Joan Beuershausen.

The rest of Charlie's estate, his separate estate, went to the Hal and Charlie Peterson Foundation, with a portion of it being held in a life estate by his brother, Hal. The Foundation received more than $1.5 million including stock in the following corporations: Peterson's Garage and Auto Company; Kerrville Bus Company; West Texas Auto Company; Kerrville Broadcasting Company (KERV Radio); C. D. Beck & Company of Ohio; Mooney Aircraft; and the National Farm and Loan Association.

Brother Hal bought Charlie's half of the farm and ranch equipment, the ranch house furnishings, and the livestock, which had also been left to the Foundation at a price of about $40,000.

Following Charlie's death, the Foundation suddenly had investment resources which would provide income to support the hospital and its other charitable gifts. What had been a wild process of digging and scratching and borrowing to launch a medical facility was now a major Foundation engaged in managing and investing assets and income for the well being of the community.

But Charlie's widow, Violet, had gone from being one of the richest women in the Texas Hill Country to being a much less wealthy woman. She was left a pensioner, although a very well-to-do one with a pension of $1,500 a month. After Charlie's death, Violet began to drink heavily, possibly from the loss of her husband and possibly from her change in status.

Beverly Sullivan recalled: "My mother really could not survive without Charlie. It was a real special relationship. I often think of it like Nancy and Ronald Reagan's relationship. They [Charlie and Violet] were such a pair. They almost didn't need anything else in their lives."

For a few years, Violet tried to live an active social life, perhaps even attempted to meet a new love for her life. In 1956 she was chosen to direct the Kerr County Centennial Association as its executive secretary. She had also been active in Community Chest fundraising.

Increasingly, though, she became a prisoner of Charlie's will. She could no longer enjoy the life she had been living as the wife of the rich Charlie Peterson on $1,500 a month. At the same time, she could not remarry without losing her stipend. She felt poor, even though $1,500 a month was considerable income in the 1950s.

Violet gradually retreated into her home. Two houses in which she lived later burned. The first fire came when Violet was asleep in the house with her mother and daughter Beverly. All three escaped without injury. The cause was never determined. The second fire claimed Violet's life as the house in which she was alone burned to the foundation. The cause was determined to be a cigarette, according to Tommy Noonan. Violet died on February 18, 1965, at the age of forty-four.

The heart troubles that plagued the Petersons also caught up with the youngest son, Joe Sid, who died at Sid Peterson Memorial Hospital on January 11, 1958, at the age of fifty-five. At the time of his death, the local newspaper wrote:

> A native of Kerrville, he (Joe Sid) had grown to manhood in the city and on the Peterson ranches on the Divide. He attended school here and also at the San Antonio Academy. He was a vigorous outdoor type of man and loved ranch life, and spent most of his time on the ranch or at his farm home, "Casa Pobre," on the Medina Road. That he was a "man's man" was evidenced by the large number of men who came from far and near to pay their respects to him as his body lay in state or to attend the funeral services. He was loyal and most generous to his friends, who loved him dearly.
>
> He was the youngest son of the late Sid C. and Myrta Goss Peterson. He had many business interests, and at the present time was operating two ranches in the Divide section, and recently oil interests had been developed on one of his ranches. When his health would permit, he was an ardent sportsman and enjoyed hunting and fishing.
>
> The love and esteem with which he was held by his fellow

> man was manifest in the masses of flowers which blanketed his bier and the large concourse of friends who went with him to his last resting place in the family plot in Glen Rest Cemetery.

Joe Sid's death left older brother Boss the last surviving member of the Peterson family. The irony was that Boss, whose health had suffered the onslaught of heart attacks and related problems for more than two decades, was the one everyone expected to die first. Now he was the last surviving son of Cap Peterson.

Above and below: *The whole community got into the act. Crowds of people participated in constructing the "park that was built in a day."*

Above: *Hal Peterson (with glasses) plays cards with business associates at Camp Eagle.*

Below: *"Important guests" around the bar at Camp Eagle.*

Chuck wagons were set up and food was prepared for the park volunteers.

Above: *R.S.T. "Rastus" Walker delivers food for the Camp Eagle hunters.*

Below: *A new and novel improvement at Camp Eagle was the heated swimming pool.*

The rustic entrance to Camp Eagle. It was originally a boys' camp before Hal and Charlie Peterson purchased the 6,430-acre tract in 1940.

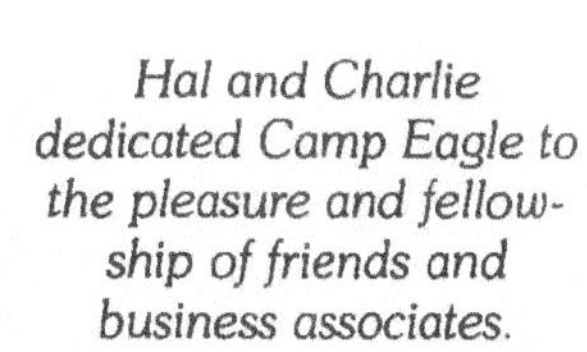

Hal and Charlie dedicated Camp Eagle to the pleasure and fellowship of friends and business associates.

Top: *Hal Peterson befriended many high-ranking military men and business associates. In photo is a general with Howard Hughes's right-hand Hollywood man, Noah Dietrich.*

Middle: *On the Peterson farm, one of Street Hamilton's daughters, Katie, with one of the Border collies.*

Bottom: *Border collies working the sheep.*

Above: *The Diamond Bar Ranch house. It was a Peterson "home on the range" before Hal and Charlie bought Camp Eagle.*

Below: *R.S.T. "Rastus" Walker entertaining at a barbecue at the Diamond Bar Ranch.*

Ringing the dinner bell at Camp Eagle.

Hal Peterson standing in front of the Diamond Bar Ranch house.

PART FIVE

The Later Years

Betty Lee, Boss's stepdaughter, with his wife Billie.
Boss became her business mentor.

CHAPTER 15

A Change of Interests

"WHEN YOU'RE TALKING, YOU'RE not learning."

George Delavan, who "looked after" Boss's developments in San Antonio, remembered that Boss frequently spoke those words. Even more significantly, he lived them.

With his long cigarette holder and his thick eyeglasses that made his eyes look even bigger than they were, Boss could listen his way through any deal.

"Boss would stare at you without blinking," said Delavan, "and you knew he was thinking about it. He looked at the man."

Like his father Cap, Boss had an eerie way of sizing up people, and he was rarely wrong.

Betty Lee Halff remembers the many deals during the 1950s that were brought to Boss and discussed across the big round table at his home on Morningside. "Boss had a sense about business negotiations that was part talent and part science," she said. "He had good, strong intuitions."

Delavan said that when a man pitched a business idea to Boss, the silence could be stunning. Boss would listen without responding. Uncomfortable, the man would talk through the plan again, this time improving the deal for Boss, only to be faced again with a pensive but uncommunicative Boss. Delavan said this process would repeat itself until Boss felt certain he had heard the man's best offer. Then Boss would dismiss the man and work the details of the deal over in his mind. If it didn't excite Boss, the man would not hear back from Boss.

The type of man who would be charged with running or "looking after" the deal was very important to Boss's style of doing business. Boss would often say: "I've always been smart enough to hire somebody smarter than me."

He needed someone else to take care of the details while he concentrated on the "big picture." Delavan and Boss meshed perfectly into the team which developed homes in the top-of-the-market Castle Hills subdivision in San Antonio.

While Delavan handled the staff, the builders, and the sales, Boss handled the big shots, navigated the political hurdles, and kept the project moving.

"Boss courted the city politicians," Delavan said. "I courted the city staff."

Delavan had not intended to work for Boss. He had heard the name Boss Peterson as early as the late 1920s, when he visited relatives in Kerrville and heard about the Westland Addition, but he never dreamed of working with him. Boss owned more than twenty businesses and liked to keep five projects going at one time. "Five subdivisions." Delavan said, "can eat a lot of cash."

Delavan's first job offer from Boss came in 1958. By default on an $85,000 note, Boss had acquired Worldwide Mapping through a banker in Fredericksburg. Boss was a friend of Delavan's father, and Boss asked Delavan to manage Worldwide Mapping for him. In a pleasant way, Delavan declined the offer. The two men courted each other for five or six months before Delavan accepted an offer to work on the Castle Hills development. Delavan and his father had previously subdivided land in San Antonio, and although Boss had experience in Kerrville, he had sought advice from Delavan's father in 1953 before he launched Castle Hills.

Boss and Sterling Brown, Jr., who was married to Nora Joe Peterson, had bought the Castle Hills land from Theo Prinz and the Prinz family in 1953. They worked out a deal to sell Boss twenty acres of land with an option for Boss to purchase fifteen to thirty acres per year. When Sterling and Nora Joe divorced, Boss hired the H. B. Zachary Company to run the subdivision until 1958, when Delavan started with Boss. His first job was to exercise the annual option with Theo Prinz.

Although it was his most famous, Castle Hills was not the first development Boss built in San Antonio. Boss developed $30,000 (in 1950s prices) houses with 1,400 square feet just north of Lockhill Selma Road. In Castle Hills, his company built $35,000 to $45,000 houses (in 1950s prices) which were 3,000 square feet.

The first project in Castle Hills sold a "ton of lots" the first week. The lots were sold on terms of 80 percent down and the final 20 percent due in one year. When the one-year notes began falling due, San Antonio went into a real estate depression. The builders wanted to give the lots back, but Boss said to Delavan, "I'll tell you what to do. Let's renew and extend the notes for an additional year, and let's take them all hunting."

Delavan said that when it came time to sell more lots the following year: "You would not believe how many home builders came to buy lots to get on the hunting list again. The hunting really did work. That was a good scheme."

Then in the early 1960s, Boss built 3,500-square-foot houses in Castle Hills Estates that were the upper end of construction at that time. Today these houses bring $250,000 to $500,000.

"It was a very risky venture," said Delavan, "in that we were hitting the top notch of the market. You had to be very wealthy to build a 3,500-square-foot house in those days."

"Boss had an extraordinary amount of courage where business was concerned," said his stepdaughter Betty Lee. "He really was a venture capitalist. And I'm not sure I knew that word during the 1950s, but I know it now. He was willing to take a business risk—all kind of risks, but business in particular."

Delavan said Boss would design a subdivision in the fall, and then take everyone hunting who needed to be courted during the winter. Then Boss would sell the subdivision in the spring.

"Boss contributed an awful lot of good ideas, and it was my job to carry them out," Delavan said. "Some of the ideas I thought were way out there, and we would never be able to make them go."

As an example, Delavan cited an advertising program Boss dreamed up. Boss would pay for half of a builder's ad if the builder would also list all other builders in the project and include a map of how to get there. Despite Delavan's doubts, the advertising program was overwhelmingly successful.

But both Delavan and Frank Stanush believe that one business contributed to Boss's final decline in health. The mapping company that Boss had taken over, against the advice of friends, was the one business failure they witnessed.

"I begged him not to get into that business," Stanush said. "Boss got into it one night, and it contributed very much to his health troubles later. He would worry about it in bed. It was such a complex business. It had airplanes flying all over the world mapping for the government. And the government was very delinquent in paying its bills. It took much more capital than Boss intended. I tried my best to help boss salvage that company. That was the only big mistake I saw Boss make. He misjudged that one."

Even though he lived in San Antonio, Boss continued to journey to Kerrville on weekends for business parties at Camp Eagle.

Throughout his life Boss kept trying to do things for Kerrville. In the 1950s, the nation searched to locate an air force service academy like West Point for the army or Annapolis for the navy. Boss thought Kerrville should be the site, and he worked tirelessly to pull off the politics needed to land that academy. Eventually, the air force narrowed the choices down to two locations, Kerrville and Colorado Springs. In the end, Colorado Springs prevailed, and the Air Force Academy sits just north of that mountain foothill city in Colorado. But Boss came very close to locating the academy in Kerrville.

In his final years, Boss lived with his caring wife, Billie, at 101 Morningside in Terrell Hills of San Antonio, but they had a lot reserved in Castle Hills Estates across from George Delavan's home. They had planned to build a home on that lot.

Delavan said Billie was instrumental in keeping her husband's interests functioning as his health declined. When Boss went into a near-coma for five weeks in 1958 and was unable to sign anything, Billie signed for him. "She had the same handwriting," Delavan said.

"Periodically, Boss would feel like he could not live much longer," Delavan said.

When Boss went to church, it was difficult to grab him by his coat sleeve and pull him away, not because he was particularly religious but because he liked to talk to everyone he could.

With a captain like Guy Griggs and lieutenants like Charlie Johnston at the auto company and J. D. Mahaffey at the bus company manning the helms, the businesses of Peterson Interests continued to thrive and prosper even though their leader's health problems forced him to be less involved.

The Hal and Charlie Peterson Foundation's investments soon became less tied to Peterson Interests. Having received Charlie's portion of the businesses following his death, the Foundation had to sell its interest in Peterson's Garage and Auto Company in March of 1954, when General Motors made it clear that it would not franchise the dealership if any part of it was owned by a Foundation. Foundation minutes described the transaction like this:

> Information has been furnished by General Motors that it has been their policy since 1946 that they will not issue "selling agreements" to any organization owned or controlled in any way by a Foundation, a widow, or trustees of an estate. This being a fact, it becomes necessary that this Foundation dispose of its stock in the Petersons' Garage and Auto Company or else sell the assets of Petersons' Garage and Auto Company, which would mean a loss to the Foundation as well as to Hal Peterson, the owner of the balance of the stock. . . .
>
> Due to the excessive amount of assets in the Petersons' Garage and Auto Company, amounting to approximately $600,000, it would be impossible to find a purchaser for the entire company. It would not seem fair or reasonable that the Foundation would make any move not considered fair and reasonable to the interest of Hal Peterson. . . .
>
> Therefore on a motion by Claud Gilmer, seconded by W. G. Garrett, Jr., it was unanimously voted to sell the Foundation's stock in Petersons' Garage and Auto Company to Chas. H. Johnston and Hal Peterson under the terms of the contracts with each of them that are attached to the minutes of this meeting.

The auto company was totally purchased by Johnston in July of 1962, after the Foundation again became owners of the company stock upon Boss's death.

In June of 1954, the Foundation sold its stock in the C. D. Beck Bus Company back to the company for $50,000 for the company and $75,000 for the land.

In March of 1956, the Foundation sold its part of KERV Radio at the same time Boss sold his shares.

And in December of 1960, when Kerrville was debating a heated school bond issue, the Hal and Charlie Peterson Foundation donated its half of 108 acres to the City of Kerrville for a new school, and Boss sold the remaining land for the site to the city at a price far below market value. The site faced Highway 16 on the north adjoining the Kerrville Municipal Golf Course. The venture allowed the city to expand the golf course, and the part of the city's purchase price was covered by swapping twenty-five acres of land located between Louis Schreiner Airport and the Peterson Stock Farm.

More importantly, it gave the Kerrville Independent School District the land for a new school facility. The Kerrville junior high school was named the Hal Peterson Middle School in honor of Hal "Boss" Peterson.

Outside of the Foundation and the hospital, which bear the Peterson name, the school became the only institution named specifically for Hal Peterson and is the only tribute that the leadership of Kerrville ever extended to Boss.

Like so many larger-than-life Texans, Boss wasn't one to blow his own horn. He never sought thanks or credit for anything he did. When he arranged events like the hospital dedication, he made sure the spotlight would be directed elsewhere. An associate in the last days of his life asked Boss why Kerrville had never had a testimonial dinner or honored him in any way. The associate said Boss looked kind of sad and replied, "I don't know. I've wondered that myself."

CHAPTER 16

The Maximum of Their Means

WHEN THE COLD CHILL of death begins to envelop one's body, an instinct from within wants to go home.

With Boss Peterson's health growing ever worse, Boss and Billie left San Antonio and tried to retire to Camp Eagle in late 1961 to be again a part of the rocky earth that was his heritage.

But a blood clot in Boss's leg took him back to the hospital. The doctors made an effort to remove it, but it got away from them.

Boss died on the operating table at Nix Hospital in San Antonio on March 14, 1962. He was sixty-three years old.

Dr. Kopecky, who treated Boss for twenty-seven years, said: "When you have many heart attacks—I think he had three that we knew of—you are susceptible to clots forming in the bottom of the heart and breaking off. It is called mural thrombosis. And that's what happened to Boss. A clot came loose and landed in the femoral artery. Dr. Al Hartman had Boss on the operating table removing the clot when Boss's heart stopped, and we couldn't revive him. He died very suddenly 'with his boots on.' "

Widow Billie stayed overnight with Boss's body at the Smith Funeral Home in Kerrville because, she said, "He never liked to be alone."

Services were held at First Methodist Church. Marion Smith, Street Hamilton, Frank Stanush, R. S. T. Walker, and Milton Pampell were among the list of pallbearers. In the *Kerrville Mountain Sun*, the obituary began, "A pall of sadness was cast over the city when the news of the death of Hal Peterson was learned." It went on to say, "One of his favorite projects in the last few years was the establishment of a Student Loan Fund to help deserving students attend school. This was operated through the Hal and Charlie Peterson Foundation."

One friend was quoted, "If it was something to help Kerrville, Boss Peterson did it."

Remembering her husband's funeral, Billie said, "There were so many people and there were so many flowers that we had to distribute them around to the other graves." Boss was buried next to Charlie in Glen Rest Cemetery in the Peterson family plot.

As Charlie had done, and as the brothers had obviously agreed, Boss left the bulk of his $3 million estate to the Hal and Charlie Peterson Foundation. The executors of his will were Guy Griggs, Chas. Johnston, and J. D. Mahaffey.

The will dated September 9, 1960, contained a signed "acceptance under will" by his widow, Mildred "Billie" Ligon Peterson. Billie received more than $150,000 in insurance money and $40,000 to relinquish rights to the homestead. A trust was also established for her which amounted to about half a million dollars in assets. There was no requirement that she remain unmarried, and Billie married again later in San Antonio.

Also named in the will were R. S. T. Walker, forty-five, a resident of Kerr County. Rastus, who was a witness to Boss Peterson's will, received $1,200. Trusts of $6,000 each were established for Dundee Murray, four, and Melissa Murray, two, of Bexar County, who were Billie's grandchildren by her daughter Betty Lee.

And, of course, the Hal and Charlie Peterson Foundation in Kerr County received the bulk of the estate which was estimated to be worth $2,164,563 after all expenses and taxes were paid.

The assets included loans that Boss had made to many people and small businesses, all of which totaled close to $400,000.

The corporate stocks included assets in First City National Bank of Houston, worth $46,110; Halbart Company of San Antonio, worth $100,770; Yellow Cab Company of Kerrville, worth $1,804; Kerrville Bus Company, worth $665,387; Petersons' Garage and Auto Company, worth $373,000; West Texas Auto

Company, worth $77,124; Beverly Studios, worth $40,000; Modern Builders, worth $28,958; Products Lumber and Supply Co., worth $17,690; Chas. Schreiner Bank, worth $10,000; Castle Investments Corp., worth $22,500; and Lone Star Beer Distributing Co. of Lubbock, worth $3,000.

Real estate included the Beverly Studios property at 2015 N. Main in San Antonio; 6,465 acres at Camp Eagle; 3,453 acres at Peterson Stock Farm; and 12,692 acres at Taylor Ranch. All of these were estimated to be worth about a quarter of a million dollars.

Land for resale at the Castle Hills development in San Antonio added another quarter of a million dollars. After Boss's death, Delavan hosted a visit by the three executors of the estate, who knew little of Peterson's development business in San Antonio. Delavan tried to explain the five subdivisions which were being developed at once, but it was apparent to Delavan that the three businessmen did not see the picture.

"Subdivisions require a lot of cash when you go in," Delavan tried to explain, "and about halfway through, they begin to flat line, and then at the end, it's just like the lottery. Money runs in all over the place. Fortunately, we had one of those subdivisions in that payoff position. About every two weeks, I would send a $50,000 check up to Guy Griggs. He didn't know where all this money was coming from. Later, Guy admitted that when the three came down to San Antonio, it 'just went over my head.' The bus business was so different from the subdivision business. As Guy said: 'No money, no ticket. But subdivisions were sold on time.'"

Delavan asked the executors if they wanted to have a "fire sale" to liquidate Boss's investment or to continue on. Fortunately for the Peterson Foundation, the executors elected to go on with Boss's plans.

The Foundation held the stock in the subdivision until 1968, about three years before the subdivision was completed. Delavan and the development corporation bought the stock back to prevent the Foundation from facing tax problems.

Delavan said Boss was "well known in San Antonio, especially by the charities." Many charities called after Boss died, including one which had been anticipating a $50,000 gift, he added.

Between Hal and Charlie, the two brothers had bequeathed

estates totaling almost $3.4 million to their Foundation. But even more amazing, the brothers had already contributed some $2 million in non-estate money to the Foundation by the time of Boss's death.

Usually men who give millions are worth hundreds of millions, or perhaps even billions. Hal and Charlie gave a sum that was almost three quarters of their net worth before they died.

Hal and Charlie were not that wealthy. But they wisely and generously endowed Kerrville and the Texas Hill Country with a gift to the maximum of their means.

Billie Peterson's Beverly Studios photo.
She was Hal "Boss" Peterson's third wife.

Top: *Hal "Boss" Peterson with brother and partner Charlie Peterson.*

Bottom: *Joe Sid Peterson with brother Hal at a family barbecue.*

Above: *Bride Nora Joe greets her Uncle Boss.*

Below: *Nora Joe Peterson's wedding photo with her first husband Sterling, who was a business partner of Boss in San Antonio's Castle Hills Development. Joe Sid and Mary Peterson at right.*

Above: *Boss and Billie Peterson's wedding photo with friends.*
Below: *Edna and Guy Griggs at John and Beverly Sullivan's wedding.*
Beverly is Charlie Peterson's stepdaughter.

Boss entertaining at 101 Morningside in San Antonio.

Above left: *Boss Peterson in his home at 101 Morningside in San Antonio, sitting at his "round table."*

Above right: *Boss's wife Billie Peterson—always the "gracious hostess."*

Above: *Left to right: W. C. Fawcett and Frank Stanush, two of the Peterson Interests lieutenants.*

Bottom left: *R.S.T. Walker cleaning ashtrays for the chain-smoking "Boss."*

Bottom right: *Boss Peterson with his stepdaughter (Billie's daughter) Betty Lee Halff.*

Top: *One of the final photos of Boss Peterson with his wife Billie sitting on his beloved Camp Eagle patio.*

Middle: *Boss's final days were spent with Billie at Camp Eagle.*

Below: *Boss's casket and flowers at Glen Rest Cemetery in Kerrville, Texas.*

The Hal and Charlie Peterson Foundation office located in Kerrville, Texas.

Afterword

JUST AS HAL AND CHARLIE had the ability to pick solid people to "look after" their various businesses when they were alive, Hal and Charlie had the same knack in death.

The two brothers left the Peterson Foundation in hands that could multiply their legacy in the almost four decades since Boss's death.

Counting the book value of the hospital, the assets left by the Peterson brothers had grown to almost $100 million at the turn of the twenty-first century.

The total value of the Hal and Charlie Peterson Foundation's assets in 1999 had grown to $53,275,000.

The ownership and operation of the Sid Peterson Memorial Hospital was in the care of the Hal and Charlie Peterson Foundation from 1944 to 1989. The Peterson brothers' vision of the hospital, with its "dedication to humanity," was to attend to the needs of the needy. After the mid-1980s, when the federal government began to pay hospitals for Medicare patients, the board members decided that the hospital did not require access to the bulk of the money that the Peterson Foundation had been providing.

On January 1, 1990, the Foundation reorganized and transferred the ownership and operation of the hospital to the new non-profit Sid Peterson Memorial Hospital. The new structure allows the Foundation to continue its support to the hospital for necessary equipment or capital projects, and expand its giving to the many and varied Texas Hill Country causes.

In 1996 this "giving" to Kerr and adjacent counties amounted to almost $2.4 million. In 1998 the Foundation's trustees reviewed sixty-five qualified applications seeking some $6 million, of which almost $2.3 million was approved and funded.

In the decade of the 1990s, the Foundation had given out more than $20 million in grants to charitable and educational organizations in Kerr County and surrounding communities.

John M. Mosty,
secretary-treasurer-manager.
— Courtesy Jody Rhoden Backdoor Studio

John M. Mosty, Peterson Foundation manager and a member of its seven-member board of trustees, said, "It is impossible to estimate the value of the charity work the hospital has done since it opened in 1949, but the dollars spent on charity would be staggering." Mosty explained that it is also not possible to determine how much money the Foundation's operation of the hospital saved taxpayers in dollars they would have otherwise been taxed. This figure cannot be computed because the hospital did not keep records of uncompensated care money. But again, the amount of savings to the residents of Kerr County would be enormous.

"The changes in the Foundation and the hospital have come," Mosty said, "because health care has changed from the time Boss first conceived the idea of a hospital.

"Boss, Charlie and Guy Griggs never dreamed that the government would be providing 75 to 80 percent of the revenue stream coming into the hospital. Private insurance provides another 15 percent, so the cash customers are virtually negligible."

The hospital had a loss of $2.7 million in the year before Medicare began paying for the care of the elderly. "The Peterson Foundation had advanced the hospital some $13 million to fund these losses, and the books of the hospital were incorporated into the Foundation," said Mosty.

The Foundation continued its support to the Sid Peterson Memorial Hospital in the decade that followed the reorganization, with almost $8.3 million going to the hospital building and equipment, hospital projects, and funds.

More than $1.7 million has gone to Schreiner College projects during the 1990s. Prior Schreiner grant requests (through 1989) had provided $572,000 for the college.

In the 1990s the Kerrville Independent School District received almost $1.3 million in grant funding. Support provided by the Foundation for the Kerrville schools since 1960 amounts to more than $2.9 million.

Before the hospital and the Foundation became two distinctly different organizations, the Foundation had invested more than $25 million in Sid Peterson Memorial. That brought to $34 million the dollars the Foundation had endowed the hospital since Boss tossed in that first $100.

Through the years, the Foundation had followed the quiet lead of its founders, Hal and Charlie Peterson, and had kept a low profile with rather anonymous offices. The Foundation was located initially in the hospital, but during the 1970s, Foundation offices moved to the Kerrville Bus Company building (now the Kerrville Police Department). When the bus company was sold in 1988, the Foundation moved to One Schreiner Center and later relocated in the Nations Bank Building.

But in 1998, the Foundation found its permanent home when they completed a new 3,000-square-foot office building at 515 Jefferson Street. For the first time in its fifty-six-year history, the Hal and Charlie Peterson Foundation became visible to Kerrville residents.

Guy Griggs was at the helm of the Foundation from the first day until he died in 1980. After his death, J. D. Mahaffey took over the post, followed by Charles Johnston in 1982, and in 1986 the current manager John M. Mosty.

"Quite frankly, what the hospital and the Foundation are today comes from Guy Griggs," John Mosty said. "Boss had the idea and the concept, but as usual, Guy Griggs took the ball and ran with it. He was a very imposing, very amazing man."

Mosty said Griggs was even more private than Boss and Charlie.

"He didn't want any sort of credit. I've heard he would not allow the Bus Company or the Foundation or anybody to pay him anything other than what a junior executive would make. He was dedicated to what he was doing, but he was very low key. I think the only time I saw Guy Griggs embarrassed was the year the Kerrville Chamber of Commerce named him 'Citizen of the Year.' I remember going to the chamber banquet and seeing how embarrassed he was when they called him up to the podium to receive his plaque," Mosty said.

The Foundation has had even fewer secretaries than its four managers. Only three people have filled that post: Willa Mae Gibson, Nancy Jackson, and currently Susan Carver.

One of the Foundation's first big community projects, outside of the hospital, came during the 1960s when Kerrville schools decided to build the Tom Daniel Elementary School. The subdivision developer decided not to extend Singing Wind Drive, which left the school without an access road. The Foundation came up with the $65,000 necessary to build the street in front of the school, and the elementary school opened on schedule.

The next big project was the Kerrville Municipal Swimming Pool in the late 1960s, and later another pool was built in the northern part of town.

Most of the Foundation's contributions to community causes have been made without fanfare and with little or no credit to the Foundation. "Traditionally, the Foundation would rather the publicity go to the causes," Mosty said, "than to the Foundation."

In recent years, the Foundation has funded projects such as: computer equipment at Center Point Independent School District, a new track at Antler Stadium, a girls' softball field for Tivy High School, an ambulance for Leakey emergency medical services, renovation of the former Kerrville Bus Company building, which is now the home of the Kerrville Police Department, improvements at Singing Winds Park, and funds for starting a nurse training program at Schreiner College.

The Foundation often grants completion money for a project or "seed money" to help launch a needed improvement. For example, the Foundation provided matching funds for a new track at Rocksprings Independent School District.

"Reductions in state and federal funding have made the Foundation's contributions to the Hill Country communities more valuable than ever," John Mosty noted.

At times, the Foundation's financial strength has been almost literally a life saver. When the City of Kerrville took control of emergency medical services, the Foundation gave $300,000, which covered the cost of four ambulances.

And the Foundation was instrumental in the launch of another Kerrville project to provide health care for the needy: the Raphael Community Free Clinic.

Sister Marge, a nun from the order of St. Francis of Assisi based in Milwaukee, Wisconsin, is the founder and operator of the free clinic. The Hal and Charlie Peterson Foundation provided $100,000 of launch money to allow the clinic to serve its lofty purpose: to serve the uninsured of Kerrville and surrounding areas.

The clinic provides services for an average of 150 people per week.

Sister Marge said the Foundation made it possible for the free clinic to open its doors. "The Foundation gave us our solid foundation," she said. "The $100,000 provided the clinic with all of our start-up costs. If the Foundation had not been so generous, the opening of the clinic would have been delayed at least another year, and the clinic would have had to apply for funding in a number of different places. If the Foundation had not given us that money, a lot of people would have been waiting for help," said Sister Marge. As of January 1, 1999, the Raphael Clinic had administered to 5,000 people.

But as proud as Hal and Charlie would be of their Foundation if they could see it today, the two brothers would be equally gratified at what the Sid Peterson Memorial Hospital has become.

The hospital now has a book value of $40 million, but its market value would be much more. The hospital has grown to 148 beds, employs the full-time equivalent of 611 employees, has more than 75 physicians on its active medical staff, and has an annual operating budget of about $40 million.

The hospital serves a six-county area which includes Kerr, Kendall, Kimble, Bandera, Edwards, and Real counties and their 65,000 residents. A major construction project completed in 1999 created a new emergency department and renovated the exterior and the first floor of the hospital, which brought an entire new look to the facility.

As a regional medical facility, Sid Peterson Memorial Hospital has most medical specialties. The hospital owns and operates four other facilities: Townhouse Resident Center for independent retirement living; the SPMH Skilled Nursing Facility on the fifth floor of the hospital for patients who no longer require acute care but still need twenty-four-hour care before going home; the Peterson Pulmonary Rehabilitation Center, an interdisciplinary program combining education and exercise in a medically supervised environment; and the Guy Griggs Professional Building, which is adjacent to the hospital and which houses physicians' offices and other related services.

Two independent, privately owned facilities are part of the complex: the Kerrville Cancer Center and the Heart of the Hills Cardiac Rehab and Osteoporosis Center.

A few miles from the central facility, the hospital also operates two health care providers: Peterson Home Care, the largest home care organization in Kerrville; and Peterson Rehabilitation and Diagnostic Services, which offers outpatient therapy and services.

Since Boss had dreamed of the hospital becoming "The Mayo Clinic of the South," he would be proud of the many honors the hospital has earned.

In 1993 the Sid Peterson Memorial Hospital was recognized as one of the top ten hospitals in the western United States in a federal study based on Medicare data. Many famous hospitals in large cities, from Houston to Los Angeles, ranked below the Kerrville hospital.

In 1998 the Texas Hospital Association singled out Sid Peterson Memorial Hospital for the association's highest honor: the 1998 Excellence in Community Service Award. The annual award recognizes one hospital for its distinguished contributions to the community. Sid Peterson Memorial Hospital was honored for its assistance and support of the Raphael Community Free Clinic in Kerrville.

Taken altogether, an amazing Texas Hill Country legacy has grown from the two Peterson brothers who were not afraid to take a risk in business—or in their charitable endeavors.

Perhaps only risk-takers like Boss and Charlie would have dared put their family name and honor behind such an ongoing risky venture as a hospital. While the two brothers never formally gambled their entire wealth, they nevertheless placed a huge bet that their resources would be able to underwrite a major medical facility and that the people of the area would support it.

Fortunately for every resident of the Texas Hill Country, it was a bet that Hal and Charlie won.

Above: *The current Hal and Charlie Peterson Foundation officers, and Susan Carver. Front row (left to right): William Cowden, Scott S. Parker, John M. Mosty. Back row (left to right): Nowlin McBryde, Charles H. Johnston, Susan Carver, James Stehling, C. D. (Dash) Peterson.*

William Cowden

Charlie Johnston

Nowlin McBryde

Scott S. Parker

C. D. (Dash) Peterson

James Stehling

All board member portraits courtesy of Jody Rhoden Backdoor Studio

Hal and Charlie Peterson Foundation

HAL AND CHARLIE PETERSON FOUNDATION BOARD OF TRUSTEES

1944–2000

Hal (Boss) Peterson	October 31, 1944	November 7, 1946
Charlie Peterson	October 31, 1944	November 7, 1946
Guy Griggs	October 31, 1944	November 30, 1980
Henry P. Burney	November 10, 1944	July 3, 1956
Claud H. Gilmer	November 10, 1944	June 14, 1961
W. Scott Schreiner	November 7, 1946	December 1969
W. A. Fawcett, Sr.	November 7, 1946	March 1951
W. G. Garrett, Jr.	March 30, 1951	Fall 1965
Dr. Andrew Edington	July 3, 1956	January 1, 1982
John D. Mahaffey	July 7, 1961	November 2, 1982
Joe W· Burkett, Jr.	November 12, 1965	February 27, 1986
Tom Murray	December 31, 1969	November 2, 1984
Chas. H. Johnston	May 25, 1973	Current Trustee-2000
William H. Cowden, Jr.	September 23, 1981	Current Trustee-2000
Judge Julius R. Neunhoffer	January 29, 1982	December 22, 1989
Fred E. Kaiser	October 8, 1982	February 23, 1988
C. D. Peterson	July 5, 1983	Current Trustee-2000
F. W· Hall, Jr.	December 18, 1984	December 22, 1989
Scott S. Parker	October 22, 1985	Current Trustee-2000
Scott Stehling	October 22, 1985	December 22, 1989
William C. Matthews	December 23, 1986	December 22, 1989
John M. Mosty	November 28, 1989	Current Trustee-2000
James E. Stehling	September 25, 1990	Current Trustee-2000
R. Nowlin McBryde	September 25, 1990	Current Trustee-2000

OFFICERS OF THE HAL AND CHARLIE PETERSON FOUNDATION 1944–2000

Officers	*Elected to Board*	*Elected Officer From*	*End of Term*
PRESIDENTS			
Hal (Boss) Peterson	10/31/44	07/23/45	11/07/46
W. Scott Schreiner	11/07/46	11/13/46	07/07/47
W. A. Fawcett, Sr.	11/07/46	07/07/47	03/51
W. Scott Schreiner	11/07/46	03/30/51	12/69
Dr. Andrew Edington	07/03/56	12/31/69	01/01/82
Chas. H. Johnston	05/25/73	01/29/82	01/20/83
Joe W. Burkett, Jr.	11/12/65	01/20/83	07/06/84
William H. Cowden, Jr.	09/23/81	07/06/84	02/23/93
Scott S. Parker	10/22/85	02/23/93	Current
VICE PRESIDENTS			
Charlie Peterson	10/31/44	07/23/45	11/07/46
W. A. Fawcett, Sr.	11/07/46	11/13/46	07/07/47
W. Scott Schreiner	11/07/46	07/07/47	03/30/51
Henry P. Burney	11/10/44	03/30/51	07/02/54
W. G. Garrett, Jr.	03/30/51	07/02/54	Fall 1965
Dr. Andrew Edington	07/03/56	10/11/65	12/31/69
John D. Mahaffey	07/07/61	12/31/69	12/18/80
Chas. H. Johnston	05/25/73	12/18/80	01/29/82
Joe W. Burkett, Jr.	11/12/65	01/29/82	01/20/83
William H. Cowden, Jr.	09/23/81	01/20/83	07/06/84
Fred Kaiser	10/08/82	07/06/84	02/23/88
Scott S. Parker	10/22/85	02/23/88	02/23/93
William H. Cowden, Jr.	09/23/81	02/23/93	Current

Officers	*Elected to Board*	*Elected Officer From*	*End of Term*
SECRETARY–TREASURER–MANAGER			
Guy Griggs	10/31/44	07/23/45	11/30/80
John D. Mahaffey	07/07/61	12/18/80	11/02/82
Chas. H. Johnston	05/25/73	11/12/82	12/31/85
John M. Mosty	01/01/86	11/28/89	Current
ASSISTANT SECRETARIES			
John D. Mahaffey	07/07/61	04/21/62	12/31/69
Joe W. Burkett, Jr.	11/12/65	12/31/69	01/29/82
William H. Cowden, Jr.	09/23/81	01/29/82	01/20/83
Fred Kaiser	10/08/82	01/20/83	07/06/84
Joe W. Burkett, Jr.	11/12/65	07/06/84	02/27/86
Chas. H. Johnston	05/25/73	07/07/86	07/02/93
Susan Carver		07/02/93	Current

Bibliography

Persons Interviewed as Resources for This Book (Listed in Alphabetical Order)

Mrs. Jeff (Viola) Boldin—Mrs. Boldin's father lived with his wife and children on the Peterson Stock Farm. Her husband, Jeff, retired as a driver from the Kerrville Bus Company.

Joe Burkett Mr. Burkett did legal work for the Peterson Interests. He was not Hal Peterson's primary attorney, but he "attended to" quite a bit of Boss's legal work in Kerrville.

George Delavan—Mr. Delavan worked for Boss Peterson on the development of the Castle Hills subdivision in San Antonio.

Mrs. W. A. (Ethel) Fawcett—Mrs. Fawcett's husband, Junior, was a cousin to Hal and Charlie Peterson. Junior Fawcett was also Hal's pilot. He also worked for the Peterson Interests.

Willa Mae Gibson—Mrs. Gibson was secretary to Guy Griggs for over thirty-five years. She also functioned as secretary for Boss (and Charlie) Peterson. Willa Mae was the first Hal and Charlie Peterson Foundation secretary.

Carson Gilmer—Mr. Gilmer's father, Claud Gilmer, was a close friend of Boss Peterson. He was from Rocksprings and functioned as an attorney for Peterson Interests. The Gilmers owned the Rockspring Telephone Company and Carson Gilmer, as a young man, helped Boss get his phone service for Camp Eagle.

Mrs. Howard (Betty Lee) Halff Betty Lee Halff was Billie Peterson's daughter and Boss Peterson's stepdaughter. Her mother was Boss Peterson's third wife.

Mrs. Street (Ruth) Hamilton—Mrs. Hamilton and her husband, Street, lived on and managed the Peterson Stock Farm. Street Hamilton was a longtime friend of Hal and Charlie Peterson. He also worked on many additional projects for the Peterson Interests.

Mary Helen (Hyde) Hutto—Mary Helen's parents (the Lee Hydes') managed ranches (including the Diamond Ranch) for Mr. Sid Peterson. Her memories of Hal, Charlie, and Joe Sid Peterson extend back to the time when she was a young girl in the 1920s.

Ben Hyde, Sr.—Mr. Hyde drove trucks and hauled horses for the Peterson Stock Farm. He was also a test fleet driver for the West Texas Auto Company.

Charles Johnston—Mr. Johnston was general manager of the Peterson's Garage and Auto Company. After Charlie Peterson died, he became part owner with Hal Peterson and eventually he bought the company. He was cousin to Dora Johnston Peterson, Boss's first wife. Mr. Johnston served as a manager of the Hal and Charlie Peterson Foundation and he is currently a board member of the Foundation.

Mrs. Jeanie Jones—Dr. Charles Jones's widow. Her husband was one of the first doctors who worked at the Sid Peterson Hospital.

Dr. Leon Kopecky—Dr. Kopecky was Hal Peterson's longtime San Antonio doctor and friend. He met Boss Peterson in 1936, when Boss was hospitalized at the Nix Hospital with his first heart attack.

Mrs. J. D. (Eloise) Mahaffey—Mrs. Mahaffey's husband, J. D., was the traffic manager of the Kerrville Bus Company and one of the executors of Boss Peterson's will.

Carl Meek—Kerrville realtor, Carl Meek worked as a salesman at the Peterson Garage and Auto Company in the early 1950s.

Gladys (Peterson) Meyers—Mrs. Meyers is a first cousin to Hal and Charlie Peterson.

John M. Mosty—John Mosty is currently manager of the Hal and Charlie Peterson Foundation. Mr. Mosty started with Peterson's Auto Company in 1954. He worked full time at the West Texas Auto Company from 1955 to 1958 before returning to Peterson's Garage and Auto, where he was business manager and corporate treasurer until 1966.

Thomas (Tommy) Noonan Mr. Tommy Noonan's father, Addis, was the primary architect of the Sid Peterson Memorial Hospital. Tommy Noonan was a young engineer and architect at the time the hospital was being built, and his father placed him in charge of construction.

Mildred Billie Ligon (Peterson) O'Daniel—Billie was Hal Peterson's third and last wife.

Mrs. Peggy (Peterson) O'Hara—Peggy O'Hara is a first cousin to Hal and Charlie Peterson.

Clyde Parker—As a young man, Clyde Parker owned a lumber company and supplied lumber for Hal and Charlie's construction projects.

Charles (Dash) Peterson—Dash Peterson is a second cousin to Hal and Charlie Peterson. His father, Carl Peterson, was part owner of the American Pure Milk Company. Dash is a board member of the Hal and Charlie Peterson Foundation.

Wesley Plant—Mr. Plant worked as a ranch hand on the Peterson Stock Farm.

Charles Schreiner III—Charlie Schreiner is the owner of the YO Ranch. His mother, Myrtle Schreiner, was a close friend of Hal and Charlie Peterson.

Mrs. Garland (Snookie) Scogin—Mrs. Scogin worked as a secretary at the Peterson Auto Company for thirty-five years.

Frank Stanush—Mr. Stanush operated (and eventually owned) Beverly Studios in San Antonio for Hal Peterson. He remained a business partner and close friend to Boss until Boss died.

Dick Staudt—Dick Staudt managed the West Texas Auto Company for the Peterson Interests.

Mrs. Martin (Cornie) Stehling—Mrs. Stehling's mother, Cornelia, was sister to Mr. Sid (Cap) Peterson. Cornie Stehling is a first cousin to Hal and Charlie Peterson.

Jim Stehling—Jim Stehling is Cornie Stehling's son and second cousin to Hal and Charlie Peterson. He is currently a board member on the Hal and Charlie Peterson Foundation.

Jimmie Stone—As a young man, Mr. Stone played cards with Mr. Sid (Cap) Peterson. He also sold liquor in Kerrville.

Beverly (Beuershausen) Sullivan—Beverly is Violet Peterson's daughter and Charlie Peterson's stepdaughter. Beverly was a pre-schooler when her mother married Charlie.

Tom Syfan—As a young man, Tom Syfan trained border collies for Hal Peterson on the Peterson Stock Farm. He became a lifelong acquaintance of Hal Peterson.

Roy Wilkinson—Mr. Wilkinson was Hal Peterson's barber in San Antonio from 1952 to 1962 (the year that Hal died).

Mrs. Albert (Charlotte) Wolfmueller—Mrs. Wolfmueller and her husband, "Wolf," were close social friends of Guy and Edna Griggs.

Bill Womack—Bill is a second cousin to Hal and Charlie Peterson. As a young boy, he lived with his grandmother, Cornelia (Big Mama) Peterson Fawcett. "Big Mama" was Mr. Sid (Cap) Peterson's sister.

Index

The Authors

Vicki J. Audette retired from her television career in St. Paul, Minnesota, in 1990 and relocated to Kerrville, Texas, to become a full-time writer. Her interest in Hal and Charlie Peterson began with the discovery of an old Camp Eagle booklet found at Wolfmueller's books in downtown Kerrville. As a former TV reporter with a readiness for research, Vicki was enchanted by the brief glimpse into the colorful life of the Peterson brothers. Years later, when Hal and Charlie Peterson Foundation commissioned the Hal and Charlie book, she became an eager collaborator. This is Vick Audette's fifth book.

A former publisher of the *Kerrville Mountain Sun*, author **J. Tom Graham** is currently chief operating officer of Westward Comminications LLC, a Houston-based company with operates seventy newspapers in four states. Graham is the author of *Quaint We Ain't, A Weekly Editor Confesses the Truth About Small Town Life*. He also has written several plays, including *Quaint We Ain't* and a comedy entitled *For Married Only*.

www.ingramcontent.com/pod-product-compliance
Lightning Source LLC
LaVergne TN
LVHW010616100826
845148LV00014B/2988

9781681792156